I Was Thinking . . .

Musings and Meditations from a Lawyer,
Mega-Church Pastor, and General Do-Gooder

STAN BUCKLEY

WESTBOW
PRESS®
A DIVISION OF THOMAS NELSON
& ZONDERVAN

Scripture quotations are taken from THE HOLY BIBLE, NEW INTERNATIONAL VERSION®, NIV® Copyright © 1973, 1978, 1984, 2011 by Biblica, Inc.® Used by permission. All rights reserved worldwide.

WestBow Press books may be ordered through booksellers or by contacting:

WestBow Press
A Division of Thomas Nelson & Zondervan
1663 Liberty Drive
Bloomington, IN 47403
www.westbowpress.com
1 (866) 928-1240

ISBN: 978-1-9736-3763-9 (sc)
ISBN: 978-1-9736-3764-6 (e)

Library of Congress Control Number: 2018910016

Print information available on the last page.

WestBow Press rev. date: 08/24/2018

To Jewell

Contents

Introduction

In 2012, I began posting devotional thoughts on social media and emailing them to friends. Because the devotionals were centered on what I was thinking at the time, I decided to entitle them, "I was thinking . . ."

Many of the thoughts are based on the amazing work But God Ministries is doing in Haiti and the Mississippi Delta. We have seen God change countless lives as churches have been built, thousands of patients have been treated, over 130 houses have been built, wells have been dug, children have been educated, and jobs have been created. I am inspired daily by the work of our American and Haitian team members. In addition, the thousands of people who have gone on mission trips with us have inspired me in countless ways.

Other thoughts are based on my role as a husband, a father, and a son. Some thoughts are from the years I served as a pastor. God has allowed me to experience Him in various roles and in different ways and my goal has been to simply share His love and His grace and His goodness through the written word.

The more I wrote, the more determined I became to simply share what was on my mind and my heart. I wouldn't write to please any particular person. I would not argue about what I wrote. I would not defend what I wrote. I would simply share what was on my mind. If people enjoyed it, that would be great. If not, that would be OK as well. I would simply share my thoughts as honestly as I could.

After several years of writing and posting, I realized I had amassed hundreds of these devotionals. A number of people asked if I would compile them into a book. I decided to do so with the hope that someone might be inspired and encouraged.

Her name is Jayne. She walked into the holding room at the clinic where my dad was sitting in a wheelchair. He was not in good shape. He was hurting from a fall he had experienced an hour earlier in which he hit his head. He was weak from rheumatic fever, and because of the appointment, he had had nothing to eat or drink since the previous day.

Jayne saw him sitting in the wheelchair. He was hurting, he was staring straight ahead, and he was moving very little. She made small talk. She smiled. She laughed. Then, she asked if he wanted a cup of coffee since our plans were changing and he would be going to the hospital. My dad drinks a cup of coffee every morning. Has for years. He told Jayne he would love a cup of coffee. She said, "I don't drink coffee but I know where the coffee pot is. I'll have to make some but I'll be glad to do it." Soon, Jayne returned with a cup of coffee. It was exactly what my dad needed.

Then she said, "I'm just around the corner. You call me if you need anything. I'll check on you." And she did. She showered him with kindness and humor. She brought him a bottle of water. She looked after him. She looked after him even though he would not be getting a scan in her department and he was taking up space and the clinic would get nothing from his presence. Jayne was just what he needed.

His name is Michael. He works in the appliance department at a building supply store. We went there last week looking for a washing machine and a dishwasher. My parents' washing machine was 51 years old. Yes, it was a Maytag and still worked on one setting. The dishwasher was 30 years old.

Michael helped us select the proper appliances and then we talked about delivery. If both were in stock, they could have delivered them that day at no charge. But one had to be ordered. The policy would not allow them to make two deliveries without a charge. I wasn't sure what to do.

Finally, Michael looked up and said, "Where do they live?" I told him. "He said, "I'll take it to their house on my truck during my lunch break. My lunch break is at 4:00 and I'll bring it then."

I hardly knew what to say. Michael, who did not know us, was going to use his break to deliver a washing machine with his truck and his gas. And he did. Several hours later, Michael pulled into the driveway. With zero fanfare, he backed his truck into the garage, helped unload the washing machine, and helped move it to the appropriate place.

What Michael did was a big help, but it was bigger than he knew. You see, Michael had no idea we had just spent a week in the hospital with my dad, and he had no idea my mom just had double mastectomy surgery. He didn't know they had spent the night in rooms next door to one another at the hospital. He didn't know we had been dealing with countless doctors, nurses, and administrators. He didn't know we had been off work almost two weeks. He didn't know we had spent days working in the home where my parents had spent the last 30 years and we were exhausted. He didn't know the last thing we needed was another complicated situation. He didn't know any of that.

But Michael, like Jayne, chose kindness. He chose helpfulness. He chose to go the extra mile, to do more than the minimum, and to treat people with dignity and respect. I'm not in charge of that clinic or that building supply store. But if I were, I'd have Jayne lead a class on compassion. I'd have Michael teach a seminar on Customer Service.

And I'd give them both a raise.

It's not necessary. You don't have to do it any longer. You don't have to be defined by your past. You don't have to live in your past. You don't have to be controlled by your past.

What happened to you? What has defined your life for so long? Was it sexual abuse, physical abuse, divorce? Were there mean girls or bullies? Were you excluded from the in-crowd in school? What was it?

Were you abandoned by your father? Raised in poverty? Were you fired? Did your business fail? Did he tell you that you would never amount to anything? Did she call you a loser? Did they say you were too dumb or too ugly, too heavy or too thin? What was it that hurt you so much? What has controlled your life for so long?

Whatever it was, here's what you need to know: they were wrong. Dead wrong. No-doubt-about-it wrong.

I know. I know they were wrong. And I know you don't have to live your life based on something that happened in the past. Here's how I know. I know because of who He is and how much He loves you. You are a son of the King. You are a daughter of the Most High God. You are so important and so valuable that this great God spared nothing to redeem you, to bring you into the family.

And He didn't create you so you could sit on the sidelines. He's given you a personality, gifts, and abilities. You may never be the president of the company or the leader of the group, but that's OK. It really is. He created you to be you. And that's enough. He didn't create you to be me, or him, or her. He created you to be you and to live and to love and to work . . . as you.

You see, you don't have to be the fastest or the strongest to make a difference in someone's life. You don't have to be the wealthiest to help the hurting. You don't have to be the most beautiful to share someone's burden. You just have to be you, the you He created you to be.

And don't ever, ever, forget this: He loves you. He really, really, loves you. Let that soak in. You are loved with an incredible love by an incredible God.

The great Apostle Paul prayed that his friends would "grasp how wide and long and high and deep is the love of Christ, and to know this love that surpasses knowledge – that you may be filled to the measure of all the fullness of God."

When you finally realize just how much He loves you, and when you really believe it, then you're free. You're free from the burdens of the past, free from the hurtful comments, free from the paralyzing fear, free from the need to please others. You're free – wonderfully, beautifully, finally, free.

It's time. It's time for a new beginning. It's time to let go of the past, turn the page, and start a new day. God has marvelous things for you, but you can't take hold of them while holding on to the hurt and pain of the past.

So today, believe Him and not them. Reject their hurtful words and embrace His endless love. Today is a brand new day. Today, you are free.

Why don't you do it? You've been talking about it for years. You've thought about it and studied it and dreamed it. You even jotted some ideas down on that piece of paper you stuffed in the drawer. So finally, it's time. It's time to write that book. Start that project. Adopt that child. It's time to downsize. Fulfill that dream. Why not? Why not this year? Why not start that business, go on that mission trip, change someone's life? Why not?

Oh, I know. You don't have enough time. Or money. Or this. Or that. Blah, blah, blah. You never will have enough time or enough money or enough this or enough that. So stop waiting until you do. This year, not only dream that dream but start making that dream become a reality. You see, until you get started, it will remain only a dream. And dreams, as long as they remain only dreams, aren't real. They don't help anybody. They don't accomplish anything. So today, this week, talk to someone about your dream. Make concrete plans. Take the first step towards making your dream become a reality. And pray. A lot. Ask Him for wisdom and guidance and help.

I know it's a big step, and I know it's kind of scary. You probably need some encouragement. So here it is: You can do it! It will be worth it! God will help you! Others will join you! Go for it!

I'm so glad He didn't just talk about loving me and saving me and blessing me. If all He did was talk about it, I'd still be unloved and lost and miserable. But He didn't just talk about it. He loved me so much He did something about it. He left heaven, He came here, He said life-changing things, He died in my place, and He rose again defeating my greatest enemy, death. HE DID SOMETHING!

And now it's your turn. So get moving. Make a difference. And have some fun. It's going . . . to be . . . great!

Sometimes you just know. You know, you know, you know. It may be hard to explain. Words may fail you. But still, you know.

You know when it's time to make a change. Go in a different direction. Try something new. You know when you can play it safe no longer.

But it's scary. Because while you know, you don't really know. You don't know all the details. You don't know how it will work out. Or even if it will work out. But something deep inside drives you forward. Compels you to move. To act. To take a chance. You just have to. Or you will die. You'll fade into the background and do what's expected and mark the time. And it will be awful. Just awful.

And that's not an option. You can't settle for that. You can't take the safe route. You can't merely go along to get along. You can't. You just can't. Because there's something there. Maybe it's fear. Maybe it's hope. Maybe it's the belief that it might work out and it'll be great and it'll be challenging and it'll be life changing and it'll be worth it. Oh, so worth it.

So you do it. You quit that job. Start that business. Finish that degree. You do it. Or at least you try. And for a brief moment you soar into the heavens and you're free. You're free from the shackles of ordinary and safe and others. And it no longer matters what they say or what they do or whether they approve. It doesn't matter that you may fail. It doesn't matter that it may not work. None of it matters. Because you're doing it. And it's good and it's right. You're finally free to use your personality and your gifts and your education and your drive and your experiences. Free to try and go and do and give it a shot. You're free.

Sometimes you know. You just know.

It never gets old. Never, never, never. Over and over again, we can see it and experience it and it never gets old. Never same 'ole, same 'ole. Never boring or dull. Never.

Oh, lots of things do get old. Your favorite food, favorite song, favorite friend. Sometimes you just need a break. Do something different. But this other . . . never.

Changed lives. That's what I'm talking about. There's nothing like it. Seeing that struggling person go from despair to hope, from defeat to victory, from a frown to a smile. It's awfully good. Awfully fun. Gives you that warm-all-over feeling.

In Haiti we get to see it all the time. We see God's children go from a tent to a house, from sick to healthy, from broke to employed. We see people living in absolute poverty and hopelessness move to a new home and a new job and a new life.

There's St. Vierge and her new job. The first time in her 40 year life she's ever been paid. For anything. There's Junior and his new bride, married in our new church two weeks ago. There's Gabby and his full-time job. Said he receives incredible respect from his family because he gets paid every month. There's Macquil and his many opportunities to work and make a living and provide for his wife and 7 children.

There's Jacques and his newly formed construction company. He's the boss, the owner, the caller-of-the-shots. No longer a hired hand. He's a Haitian man who has a Haitian company that hires Haitian workers and buys Haitian supplies and builds Haitian buildings in a Haitian community. Lots of changed lives.

There's the one guy who left his mountain village at 2:00 a.m., walked five hours to our clinic and had five teeth pulled because he was in great pain. There's the little twin boy who was starving because his mother's milk dried up. Now he's happy and content and growing because his mother received powdered milk at the clinic.

And then there was the lady who had a temperature of 104. Would have died and left her 17 day old child. But she got help. Treatment at the clinic. She's doing great.

There are those 6 women painting and those other 6 women making clay figures. Selling them to American teams. Adding much needed cash to their families' income and helping provide food and clothing and the basics of life.

There's Orel and his wife. Moved into their new home last week from a makeshift home where they had lived for over 3 years after their house was destroyed in the earthquake. They just wanted a chance. A shot at a better life. In a good place, a safe place, a hope-filled place.

And the children. All those children. Attending school. Learning to read and write and do math. Preparing for a better future. A future fueled by scholarships from people who cared.

No, it never gets old. Never, never, never. But there's one thing to know. Haiti is not the only place where you can see changed lives. Turns out, there are people in America, in my state, in my community who need a little encouragement, a little hope, a little word to know they can make it. They're in your community, too. They just need to know someone cares. That someone will listen and understand and maybe give them a hand up. Then, just maybe, their lives can change too. And if that happens, and if you get to be part of it, you too will see that a changed life . . . never gets old.

What is it? What do you really want to do? You know, if you weren't scared. If you weren't scared what others might think. If you weren't worried what others might say.

What would you do? Where would you live? What would you say?

Would you write? Or paint? Or build or speak or travel? Would you open that business, finish that degree, start that ministry? What would you do, if you could do anything?

Would you stay? Would you go? Would you share your feelings, confess your love? What do you really want to do?

And why don't you? What's holding you back? Is it fear? Fear of failure or fear of criticism? Fear of being rejected or misunderstood? Is fear keeping you from doing or going or trying?

What do you want to do? What gives you joy and life and energy? What could you be really good at if only you would try?

What do you really, really, really want to do? Do that.

Better hurry. Not much time left. In fact, it's almost over. I don't like that it's almost over. Scares me sometimes. But it's true. One day we are young, playing with friends, not a care in the world. The next day we have exceeded the halfway point of our lives and we are shocked to discover time never stops.

What to do with this realization? I could be sad. Or distraught. Or shocked. I could give up and believe the Shakespearean line that, "Life is a tale told by an idiot, full of sound and fury, signifying nothing." I could become despondent, shrink from life, and live in hopelessness and despair.

Or I could live. Each day really live. I could decide that my years on this planet will matter. They will count because I will live them for Him and He will use them in ways I never dreamed. I could believe that my words and deeds will make a difference, both now and forever. I could invest my education and training and experience in the lives of others and see their lives changed for the better.

I could believe these short years are not the end but only a brief part of my existence. That eternity awaits and I get to spend it with Him. And them. The heroes of the faith. And the anonymous ones who just loved Him and followed Him. And those who have encouraged me to know Him and serve Him. Those I have loved and who have loved me.

I could decide that it's not over here until He decides it's over and in the meantime I keep loving and praying and working and serving. I could find great joy in the time I do have and look forward to that Great Reunion in the sky.

Give up? Lie down and quit? Not a chance.

She's right. I don't even know who she is. But she's right. She responded somewhere on social media to someone's difficult circumstances, wrote about her own, and concluded, "We are all a mess."

She's right. We're all a mess. Some of us are a bigger mess than others, but we're all a mess. Some of us are a mess right now and all of us have been a mess in the past. We're all a mess.

Some of us are a physical mess. We've received the diagnosis. We're going through treatment. The prognosis is bad. The pain is constant. We're a mess.

Some of us are a financial mess. The bills keep coming. The pay has been cut. The savings are gone. There's more month left than money. We're a mess.

Some of us are a relational mess. The marriage is unraveling. The kids are out of control. Friends can't be found. We're a mess.

Some of us are an emotional mess. The nights are sleepless. Depression is real. No one understands. We're a mess.

Some of us are a spiritual mess. God seems far away. His voice isn't heard. The Bible is unread. Prayers are unsaid. We're a mess.

So what do we do? Where do we turn? What does it all mean? Maybe it means we're all in this boat together. Maybe it means everywhere we go today we'll encounter hurting people and struggling people. People who are a mess.

And maybe it means we give them the benefit of the doubt. We show a little compassion. We speak a kind word. We give a warm hug. Maybe we brighten someone's day. Relieve their burden. Share their pain. Maybe we ask and then listen. Really listen.

After all, she's right. We're all a mess.

We're like them. You and me, we're like them. We're like those great people, those heroes, those people who have made a real difference in this world. People like Moses and David, Peter and Paul, Washington and Jefferson, Churchill and Eisenhower, King and Graham. We're like them.

How are we like them? We have hands and feet, legs and arms. We have eyes and ears and fingers and toes. We have minds that think and plan and solve. We have time and opportunity. We're like them.

No, we're not perfect. We don't have superhuman strength. We can't jump tall buildings in a single bound or fly through the air or pick up heavy objects. And neither could they. We're like them.

They made a difference. They used their God-given abilities to make a positive difference in the lives of other people. They didn't have to. They could have refused to. They could have stayed on the sidelines and been lazy or selfish or scared or apathetic. But they didn't. In spite of all the obstacles, all the challenges, all the reasons they couldn't do it, they did it anyway.

Maybe you're thinking you would like to but you can't do it alone. Can't make it happen by yourself. Then join a group, a club, a church, an organization that's making a difference. Add your strengths and your talents and your resources to what they are doing. Encourage, advise, give, help. Do it with them.

And if you're part of a group that's supposed to be doing something but is really doing nothing, get out. As fast as you can. Go. Find somebody that's doing something that's making a difference and become part of their group. Life is a vapor. We have only a short time to make a difference. A very short time.

So stop doing nothing. Stop wasting all that time watching television, surfing the internet, and pursuing pleasure. Instead, do something. Do something that matters. Do something that makes a difference in the lives of other people. Watching television, surfing the internet, and pursuing pleasure do not make a difference in the lives of other people. They just don't.

I am convinced. With every fiber of my being, I am convinced. I am convinced that people like you and me can make a difference. We really can. After all, they did. And we're like them.

Do something. DO something. Do SOMETHING. DO SOMETHING. Get up, get going, and do something. Oh, not for you. Or me. Do something for children who are hungry, families who are living in tents, women who cannot read or write, men who have no jobs to support their families. Do something. With what, you ask? With your time and your talent and your treasure. Do something with you. Your person. Your self. You. After all, you have much to offer.

Stop protesting. I know you don't speak multiple languages and you haven't mastered every aspect of Christian theology and you've never conducted surgeries in a jungle. But you have a heart for the poor. You really do want to help the suffering. You want to see lives changed. So do something.

You have time. Just as much as everyone else. Those two hours of television watching each day amount to 14 hours each week that could be used for greater purposes. Use that time to volunteer, to invest in hurting people, to think and plan and research and organize. Use that time to make a difference. All that internet surfing is helping no one. So spend your time on something that matters and that shares God's love with a desperate, hurting world.

You have talent. Yes you do. Your talent would include your education, work skills, family background, life experiences, relationships. Also, that get-it-done attitude. What could you do? Well, what do you want to do? Where are your interests? Explore those and see how God has wired you and then use those interests and skills as a road map to service.

You have treasure. The truth is that if you make $50,000 per year, your income is higher than 99% of the people of the world. Congratulations! You're wealthy and you didn't even know it. So give. A lot. Spend less on self and more on others. It will be a lot more rewarding than buying yet another trinket for yourself or your family. In fact, give so much that it hurts. That it's a sacrifice. That you are unable to buy something else or do something else because you are giving so much for the glory of God and the benefit of others. Can we honestly say with King David, "I will not sacrifice to the Lord my God burnt offerings that cost me nothing" (2 Samuel 24:24).

So what's the hold-up? Get going. There are hungry people who need food. Sick people who need medicine. Lonely people who need a friend. Hurting people who need comfort. Homeless people who need shelter. Lost people who need Jesus. And God has a plan. That plan is YOU! That plan is ME! Have fun and DO SOMETHING!!

It doesn't matter. Not one bit. It makes no difference. None of it. Those things we worry about and get angry about and spend time on. They don't matter.

My house is not in perfect order. My favorite team lost. My friends/ neighbors/people-I-just-met have a better job or a nicer car or a smarter husband or a prettier wife. She talked about me or ignored me or didn't invite me. He cheated me on that business deal. It doesn't matter.

Most of the things in our churches don't matter. You know, those things we spend much of our time and energy on. The color of the carpet. The budget. This committee, that committee. Whose feelings are hurt. Which song we like, which song we don't like. Who's in charge. How long the service was. It doesn't matter. It just doesn't.

Some guy named Solomon, who was supposed to be really smart, said that it's all meaningless, a chasing after the wind. All the pleasure and all the wisdom and all the work and all the wealth. Meaningless. That's what he said. It's in the Bible. Ecclesiastes.

So it's all meaningless. All of it. Well, almost all of it. It's all meaningless except for your spouse. Your spouse matters. And your children and your mom and your dad. They matter. They matter a lot. Just ask someone whose spouse or children or mom or dad are no longer here. Ask them. They'll tell you all that other stuff – the job promotion, the clean house, the fancy cars, the church squabbles – those things don't matter. They're a chasing after the wind.

And there's one other thing that matters. Him. He matters. He's great and mighty and good and kind. He cares and He loves. He always has been and He always will be. He's the Great I Am. Our Rock and Fortress. Our Shield and Deliverer. He's our Ever-Present Help in Times of Trouble. He is the Ancient of Days, the Lord of Hosts, and the Most High God. He is Abba Father and He matters. Boy, does He matter.

I hope to figure it out in this year. For years I've messed it up, gotten it backwards. I've focused on those things that don't matter and I've neglected those things that do matter. I hope to get it right this year. After all, most of it . . . just doesn't matter.

Here we go again. Another new year. Twelve months spread before us. Fifty-two weeks of opportunity. Three hundred sixty-five days to make a difference. What will we do with this possibility? How will we treat this great opportunity given to us by God?

Will we waste it on the frivolous? Will we spend it on the selfish? Will it be all about us and ours and what we can get and what we can do and what we can accomplish? Will it be all about us?

Or, at the end of this year, will anyone's life be better because of what we've done and how we've lived? Will the despondent be encouraged? Will the jobless be employed? Will the homeless be housed? Will the ignorant be educated? Will the hungry be fed? Will the lost be found? Will anyone's life be better as a result of our actions and our words and our lives? Anyone?

I've learned there are a lot of "anyones" out there. There are a lot of hurting and hopeless people who just need a little help, a little encouragement, a little something to get them on the right track. They just need someone to believe in them and tell them they can do it. They just need to know they are not alone and someone cares. They need to know God cares. He really does. They just don't know it. Someone should tell them. And then show them.

Of course, it won't happen by accident. We are busy people. We are active people. We have full calendars with places to go and people to see. So, we must decide to make a difference. We must make a plan to make a difference. We must partner with others to make a difference. It won't happen by accident. It just won't.

But when it does? Oh boy, when it does! When it happens, when we use our time and our talent and our treasures to invest in the lives of others, it makes all the difference. Lives are changed, including ours. Hope is born, people come alive, the future is brighter, and the world is better.

I'm thinking that this year, people in poverty-stricken Haiti and people in poverty-stricken rural Mississippi could use a hand-up. I'm thinking they could use some encouragement and some hope and some love. I'm thinking God has blessed me in ways far more than I deserve and I could use those blessings to invest in the lives of others.

It's a new year. And that's what I'm thinking.

What do you like to do? What are your skills? What is your passion? Seems like God made every one of us a certain way, with certain desires and abilities and interests. Some people like to build things. Some people like to grow things. And that's good because we need things built and we needs things grown.

Me? I hate building things and I hate growing things. Doesn't interest me. Not good at it. Don't know how. Of course, I love things once they're built and once they're grown. I greatly admire those who can build and grow. Just don't ask me to build them or grow them. One time, in 8th grade shop class, I built a bird house. The birds wouldn't even use it. Growing things? I've never even grown a tomato plant.

What do I like to do? I like to plan. And organize. I like to teach and preach and lead. I like to write. These things light my fire and get me excited. I work hard at them and love doing them. I'm a lot better at planning and organizing and teaching and preaching than I am at building and growing.

Seems like some of us in the church spend a lot of time trying to get people who like to build things to teach. We try to get somebody to do something they're not good at and don't even like doing.

Over the last few years, in Haiti, I've seen people who love children work with children. I've seen people who love construction build houses. I've seen people who are skilled in medicine treat patients. I've seen people who enjoy teaching the Word lead Bible studies. I've seen people who are talented artists teach others how to paint. I've seen people skilled in using big machinery build roads. And I've watched them love it! Come alive. Feel useful and helpful. I've seen them take their skills and abilities and passions and use them for His glory and the benefit of others. And it's a joy to behold.

What do you like to do? What are your skills? What is your passion? Do that. Do that for Him and for others. Just do that.

I want to be like him. He's this guy who is always positive, always encouraging, always uplifting. Always. For the ten years I've known him, he's been this way. Always. Every conversation. Every encounter. Every time.

And it's not just me. Turns out he's that way with everyone. I had a conversation with a mutual friend the other day who said, "he's the finest man I've ever met." I was compelled to reply, "if there's a better man walking this earth, I haven't met him."

What's his secret? Why do so many feel this way about him? I think there are many reasons, but one of the more important ones is his tongue, that tiny part of the body that is so strong and so powerful.

Somewhere along the way, he mastered it. Somewhere along the way, he realized he could use his tongue to build people up or tear them down. To be positive or negative. To uplift or destroy. And he's chosen the former. Every time.

Now don't be mistaken. He'll speak the truth. He'll speak the hard truth when it needs to be said. He'll address the tough issues. But he'll do so with wisdom and strength. He'll be calm during a raging storm. And that's why people like him. Why they want to be around him. Why they seek him out during the good times and the bad.

I think he must have read what a man named James wrote a long time ago. In fact, I'm sure of it. James wrote that the tongue is small, like a bit in the mouth of a large horse or a rudder on a big ship, but wields enormous power. He said it's like a small spark that can ignite an entire forest. That's how powerful the tongue is. That's how important our words are.

After watching this guy for a decade, I think he realized many years ago he could spend his time making a difference in people's lives and he could do so with his words. He could speak hope and joy and love into people's lives. He realized he had the option to do that. And he decided that's what he would do.

After all these years, I'm beginning to realize I have the same option. And so do you. Like him, we can speak hope and joy and love into people's lives. We can encourage and uplift and strengthen. It's a choice. He made that choice. And my life is better, far better, because he did.

All he did was write a letter. That's all. And it wasn't even his letter. He simply took dictation, wrote what somebody else said. He didn't come up with the words or the thoughts or the ideas. He just wrote what he was told to write. Some would say he wasn't very important. He wasn't famous or wealthy or brilliant or beautiful. All he did was write some words on some paper. In fact, you've likely never heard of him. Tertius. That was his name. It's a funny name.

But as it turns out, Tertius was important. Very important. The words he wrote became the theological underpinnings of Christianity. The words he wrote have been read by billions of people. The words he wrote have been memorized by children and adults around the world. The words he wrote have been proclaimed by the greatest preachers in history. The words he wrote have been used to change lives both now and forever. We call his letter Romans. It came from the mouth of Paul and through the pen of Tertius. In Romans 16:22, at the end of the letter, it says, "I, Tertius, who wrote down this letter, greet you in the Lord."

So the next time you're feeling down because you're not famous or wealthy or brilliant or beautiful, think of Tertius. Think of Romans. And remember, it's the world that values fame and wealth and brilliance and beauty. But I have yet to read the verse that calls me to be famous or wealthy or beautiful or brilliant, though none of those are bad. I have, however, read many verses that call me to be faithful and obedient and good and kind.

In fact, this one guy in the Bible wrote that we should "cling to what is good. Be devoted to one another in brotherly love. Honor one another above yourselves. Never be lacking in zeal, serving the Lord. Be joyful in hope, patient in affliction, faithful in prayer. Share with God's people who are in need" (Romans 12:8-13).

I may never be famous or wealthy or brilliant or beautiful, but I can do better than that. I can love others and I can be obedient to God and His word - that word written long ago by some guy named Tertius.

It's so strange. It's not what you would expect. In fact, it's the opposite.

I read about it this morning. A guy named Matthew described it. And it's stunning. Shocking. The intensity and the severity are not what you would expect from one who was supposed to be meek and mild. But there it was in black and white. Or red, depending on your version.

It was yet another debate/confrontation/incident between the religious folks and Him. You might call them the "church people" of their day. They went to church all the time, knew all the church rules, and looked down on those who didn't.

I know He loved them, but He didn't seem to like them very much. I suppose it's because they knew better. They had no excuse. They knew the right way to live. They knew what God desired. They had all they needed physically, socially, economically. And yet, according to Him, they were egotistical, prideful, hypocritical, legalistic, greedy, self-indulgent, blind, wicked, and sinful. Ouch.

They pranced around seeking to impress everyone with their outward piety, looking down on those who weren't as religious as them, and He didn't like it. Not one bit.

So what did He do? He called a spade a spade. He confronted their hypocrisy and then hung out with those who didn't know better, who didn't know the way, and who knew they hadn't arrived but had begun to want to. He went to their homes, sat at their tables, and shared their meals. He healed their sick and loved their lost and enjoyed their company. He loved them where they were and shared a better way.

I wish I was more like Him.

Ever been sad? Discouraged? Depressed? Like when you receive bad news or someone betrays you or the finances don't add up or you get the dreaded diagnosis. Or when work is terrible or you can't find a job or your family is falling apart.

Sometimes, things aren't good. And you can't fix them. So you're sad. You want to give up. And you would, if it were possible. You'd just quit. Lie down. Call it a day.

We've all felt that way. All of us. No exceptions. I know you think you're the only one. But you're not. You're in good company. With everyone. Who's ever lived. I know, some problems are worse than others. But I'm telling you, we've all been in that situation where we were overwhelmed with challenges and problems and trials. I may not be there now, but I've been there before and I'll be there again.

It's always been that way. After all, that's how they felt. Sad, angry, disappointed. The one they had embraced, who had given them love and hope and meaning, had been killed. And it wasn't right and it wasn't fair. But it was true. And now all the love and all the hope and all the meaning were gone. And they were sad. Terribly sad.

Until they got the good news! Until they heard the report. I read about it this morning. The report came in the form of a question. While looking for his body at the grave they were asked, "Why do you look for the living among the dead? He is not here, he has risen!" And suddenly, in a moment, in the twinkling of an eye, their sadness turned to joy. And all these years later, this amazing report still brings great joy and endless hope. Why?

There's hope because He can hear our prayers. He can respond. He can intervene.

There's hope because He is preparing a place for us where there's no more death or mourning or crying or pain.

There's hope because no matter what happens to our Christian friends and loved ones, we will see them again. For all eternity.

There's hope because death is not the end. The grave is not our final resting place. Because He lives, we too shall live.

There's hope because while our problems are merely temporary, we are not. Our problems will last a short time, but we will live forever.

There's hope because He cares for us and He sends His other followers to care for us too. To love us and help us and bless us. If we'll let them.

There's hope because everything He said is true. All the wisdom, all the instruction, all the encouragement, it's true. You can read it. You can study it. You can discuss it. And most of all, you can count on it.

He's alive! He is risen! And hope is reborn!

Sometimes, you just need some good news.

Go ahead. Do it. Stop talking about it. Stop putting it off. Do it.

You know, that thing you've been wanting to do. For a long time. You've had that dream hidden in your heart for a long time. But you haven't fulfilled it. You haven't even started.

Oh, I know. It's a little far-fetched. It's out of your comfort zone. People will say you're crazy. It's certainly not the safe route and you've got a spouse or a hamster or a hangnail so it's just not good timing.

I'm curious. What is it for you? What is that one thing you know you were created to do? That one thing for which you have the passion and the desire and the skills and the training? You could do it. If you only would.

Is it starting a business from scratch? Is it going back to school and finishing that degree? A new ministry, a non-profit, a class to teach? What is it that gnaws at your heart whenever you get still and quiet and you allow yourself the freedom to think and dream and pray?

I know, there are lots of excuses. Good ones, even. Let's deal with them. Excuse No. 1 – "I might fail." You probably will. So what, we all do. Just get back up and keep going. That's how you grow and learn and figure out how to do it.

Excuse No. 2 – "I've made mistakes and I don't deserve to have good things happen to me." Of course you don't. But what's that got to do with it? God uses flawed people to achieve great results, and He gets the glory. That's the way it works. Always has. Remember, Abraham was a liar, Moses was a murderer, David was an adulterer and a murderer, Peter was a betrayer, and Paul actually hunted down Christians and had them killed. So enough of that, "I'm not worthy," excuse.

Excuse No. 3 – "I can't do it." Who are you, Moses? That's the same excuse he used. You can do it. With determination, grit, help from friends and family as well as God Himself, you can do it. You figure it out. Along the way. You work and try and experiment. You fail and pick yourself up. You cry and pray and fret and hope. That's the way it works. If you wait until you've got it all figured out, you'll never get started.

Excuse No. 4 – "What will people say?" Who cares?!? God didn't create you to spend your life trying to please everybody but Him. In the end, it doesn't matter what they say. Most of the ones doing the talking have never accomplished their dream, so why listen to them? The naysayers should never have the final word, especially in someone else's life. Your momma or your cousin or your childhood friend may not understand your dream, but that's OK. Let that be their problem and not yours.

So go ahead. Stop reading this little devotional and do it. Start planning. Take concrete steps. Schedule a meeting with someone who can help. Sit down with someone who believes in you and will encourage you. JUST. GET. STARTED!

Run along, now. You have work to do.

Friends? Family members? Coworkers? Neighbors? Fellow church members? Former classmates? Which people are the influencers in your life? We all have people who influence us. No matter how strong or independent we think we are, we are all influenced by others.

So, the question is not whether people influence us. The question is who are the people that influence us? And in what ways?

One time Jesus told His disciples to "be on guard against the yeast of the Pharisees and Sadducees" (Matt. 16:6). He was talking about their influence and specifically their teaching. Jesus knew these religious folks exerted great influence on the minds and actions of the people. But He knew their influence wasn't good.

What about your influencers? Are they godly people? Kind people? Good people? Positive people? Optimistic people? Are they people who build you up and encourage you?

Or, are they ungodly people? Are they negative people? Are they pessimistic people? Are they people who always see the cloud in the silver lining? Are they people who tear you down and discourage you?

Over the years, God has sent incredible people into my life to encourage me. They thought I could, so I thought I could. They believed in me, so I believed in me. They thought things were going to turn out well, so I thought things were going to turn out well. They were positive, so I was positive.

Of course, there have been negative people as well. I have determined over the years that I will not allow them to be my primary influencers. Why should I? It does no good. Nothing is accomplished. They darken my mood, my outlook, and my work. There is no point in giving them access to my mind and my work and my life.

We have a choice. We can allow the negative Nellies to influence and control us or we can choose to ignore them. We can refuse to spend time with them. We don't have to be rude, but we also don't have to allow them to control who we are, what we think, or what we do.

So today, identify those positive people in your life and choose to be influenced by them. Take them to lunch. Call them on the phone. Ask them questions. Get their opinions. And today, be sure and "guard against the teaching of the Pharisees and Sadducees." You'll be glad you did!

I don't know. I wish I knew, but I don't. I feel like I should know. After all, I've been a Christian for a long time. I teach Sunday School. Preach on occasion. Even went to seminary. And I still don't know.

I don't know why some people get cancer and some don't. I don't know why tornadoes strike some homes and not others. I don't know why hurricanes rage or children starve or accidents happen.

I don't know why godly people who love the Lord and serve Him faithfully suffer from disease or job loss or divorce. It hardly seems fair. Especially when the ungodly appear to prosper.

Sometimes I just want to ask Him why. WHY? WHY HIM? WHY HER? WHY DON'T YOU DO SOMETHING ABOUT IT? Why don't you cure the disease, feed the hungry, stop the oppression? You have the power, so why don't you do it? Just do it.

I feel bad because I don't know. Maybe I'm not smart enough or spiritual enough. Maybe if I were deeper or more godly, then I would know. But I don't know. Maybe I'm the only who feels this way. I just don't know.

And that's what I'm thinking today.

Drove by yesterday. Realized I have to go there. I don't want to go there, but there's nothing I can do about it. I can't not go. I have to go. In fact, everyone goes there.

What did I pass? A cemetery. It was a bit of a jolt as I passed and realized I'll be going there and there's nothing I can do about. No way to prevent it. I'm going. And so are you.

But instead of feeling depressed, I felt a sense of urgency. I realized my time on this planet is quickly fading so I need to do whatever it is I'm called to do. Or want to do. Or should do. I need to get busy and stop procrastinating.

I can't become that old guy on his death bed wishing he would have gone for it, taken a chance, given his all. No way. Not me. Not going to be that guy. I may stumble. I may fall. I may even fail. But it won't be for lack of effort or lack of courage. It won't be because of apathy or indifference.

It's true. I'm going there one day and there's nothing I can do about it. But between now and then . . . Oh boy, between now and then, there's a lot I can do. And it's time to get busy.

Ordinary people. Like you. And me. Like your friends and neighbors. Your fellow church members. Just people. With a few gifts. A few talents. A few resources. It's ordinary people like us that God has used for thousands of years to bring about significant change. People like the boy David, the girl Mary, the fisherman Peter. As Richard Stearns wrote, "If the gospel is to be proclaimed, poverty defeated, racism overcome, the tide of AIDS turned back, or injustice challenged, it will be done by ordinary people like you and me" (*The Hole in our Gospel*).

Unfortunately, so many of us believe God could never use us, that we have nothing to offer in His service. We wrongly believe that if we were smarter, or richer, or more skilled, or knew more important people, then we could do great and mighty things for God. Sadly, we refuse to engage. We refuse to get involved. We refuse to offer what we do have to the God who fed 5,000 with 5 loaves and 2 fish.

"But," we protest, "that's just a story. It's just an ancient little tale of Jesus feeding some hungry people." No it's not! It's so much more than that. It is the perfect demonstration of how God can take that which is offered, no matter how seemingly insignificant, and do extraordinary things that make a real difference in the lives of hurting people.

But it will never happen. We will never see it. We will miss out on the Great I AM using us in extraordinary ways if we do not offer to Him what we do have. Instead of lamenting or complaining about what we do not have, we simply need to offer Him what we do have. OUR gifts. OUR talents. OUR minds. OUR efforts. OUR resources. Instead of worrying about what we don't have or wishing we had what someone else has, we should simply offer to God what we do have, believing that He will take that and do great and mighty things that we never knew.

And yet we still protest, saying, "But my gifts and talents and resources are so small, so slight, so insignificant." Remember, it's not about how small your gifts are. It's about how big your God is. Fortunately, it's about His power and His strength and His ability to make much of little.

So today, this morning, right now, let's stop focusing on what we don't have and start offering to God what we do have. Then, let's pray and work and do and believe that He will use us for His glory and the benefit of others. It's time, Christian. It's time to help that neighbor, start that ministry, work with those who are suffering, go on that mission trip, love the unlovely, minister to that hurting family, join those other Christians in that worthy cause. It's time. It's simply time. It's time to set the excuses aside, rally those other Christians, and get the job done. Then, when we do, we will experience the incredible joy of being used by Him to see lives changed now and forever. And remember. That. Never. Gets. Old!

I can't decide if it's bad. Or wrong. Or just not the best. I'm not sure. But it's the truth. A somewhat painful truth, but the truth nonetheless.

One of the strongest motivators in my life is the fear of failure. It's not the only motivator. There are many others. Good ones. But the fear of failure is strong. Very strong.

The fear of failure is so strong that I am willing to work as hard as possible for as long as possible to avoid even the hint of failure. I want no part of failure. Don't want it near me. Don't want it around me.

Why am I so driven to avoid failure? There was no pressure in my childhood to achieve. Just to do my best and give a good effort. So why does this fear of failure serve as such a motivating force?

Maybe I want others to see me as successful or smart or more-than. I certainly don't want them to think of me as a failure or dumb or less-than. That would be horrible. I think.

Maybe I want to be respected or loved and believe success will bring both. Or perhaps I want to be admired or recognized for some achievement.

This fear is strange because I know failure is part of being human. I have failed, and I continue to fail. I have failed at times in athletics, in academics, in the practice of law, as a pastor, and while founding and leading a non-profit. I have failed as a husband and a father and a friend. Things haven't always been perfect. Life hasn't always turned out as I had hoped. I know failure is real and unavoidable. But I still fear it.

So I work hard. And often. And do everything I can to avoid it. Yes, the fear of failure is real. Very real.

Don't do it. Just don't do it.

I know, it would be great. And fun. And like nothing else. But don't do it.

Yes, it's enticing. Very enticing. Intoxicating, really. But don't do it.

Of course, you deserve it. You've earned it. You're practically being forced into it. But don't do it.

Why? Because it will be fun and intoxicating. For a while. And then it won't be. Then it will be repulsive and sickening and debilitating. Then it will cause grief and heartache that you never imagined. Lives will be greatly damaged. A spouse, children, parents, in-laws, friends, church members, neighbors, people you work with—they will all be horribly affected.

I know, I don't understand. I haven't walked in your shoes. I don't know what you've put up with or what you've gone without. But don't do it.

I read some wise words this morning from the wisest man who ever lived. He was writing to his son. What he told his son was a warning. "The lips of an adulteress drip honey, and her speech is smoother than oil; but in the end she is bitter as gall, sharp as a double-edged sword."

He told his son what to do. "Keep to a path far from her, do not go near the door of her house."

He told that boy what would happen if he succumbed to the temptation. He said to stay away from her, "lest you give your best strength to others and your years to one who is cruel, lest strangers feast on your wealth and your toil enrich another man's house."

He said it wouldn't end well. "At the end of your life you will groan, when your flesh and body are spent. You will say, 'I have come to the brink of utter ruin.'"

If you're close, stop. If you're flirting with disaster, run. If you have an unhealthy relationship headed in the wrong direction, go the other way.

Cut off the relationship. Completely. Do whatever you have to do. Change jobs. Move. Report to an accountability partner. Do not continue, as the wise man said, "like an ox going to the slaughter."

It's not worth it. You think it is, but it's not.

So don't do it. Just don't do it.

What can we do? What do we say? How do we help?

It seems that lately I've faced an avalanche of difficult news. Someone is sick. Someone is depressed. Someone is bankrupt. Someone is addicted.

What am I supposed to do? I feel so helpless. I can't fix their problems. I don't have the power. I don't have the authority. I can't make everything better.

What can I do for that neighbor who is going through a divorce? That friend who is suffering from depression? That church member who received the diagnosis? That friend who lost the job?

There's nothing I can do. Or is there?

I can listen. I can smile. I can show up. I can write a note. I can write a check. I can encourage. I can laugh. I can cry. I can share Scripture. I can take a meal. I can give a gift card. I can run an errand. I can pick up kids. I can give a ride. I can pray.

No, I can't fix their problems. At least not many of them. But maybe that's not what I'm supposed to do. Maybe my role is just to be there. And love them. After all, that's what He said to do. Love one another. In a world of sorrow and pain and heartache, He just might be right.

He was crazy. A nutcase. Who acts like that? He ate bugs. That's right, bugs. Probably no ketchup to hide the taste. And he certainly wasn't voted Best Dressed his senior year. Not with that get-up made of camel's hair.

And he didn't care. He didn't care what everybody else thought or said. It wasn't his goal to conform to their expectations. He didn't care.

Actually, he did care. John cared a lot. He cared about being obedient to God and fulfilling the mission he had been given. He wanted to please God. He cared about that.

And so he spoke up and he spoke out. He told them to turn from their wicked ways. He told the religious elite they were a bunch of snakes and they couldn't count on their heritage and their endless traditions to be acceptable to God. They didn't like that, but they came to listen anyway. Lots of them. He was so on fire with the power of the Living God they couldn't stay away. Even those who hated him.

Turns out it's not those who conform and go along with the crowd and act like everybody else who make a difference in this world. Never has been. It's those who know who they are and Whose they are and what their purpose is. It's those who are willing to stand against the culture and speak the truth even when no one wants to hear the truth. It's those who refuse to be intimidated and pushed to the side and dismissed. It's those who are willing to stand for what is good and right and true even if they have to go it alone. Seems like our world today could use a few more folks like John.

I like him. I like John. And while he sought the approval of no man, he received the ultimate approval when that guy named Jesus said, "Among those born of women there has not risen anyone greater than John the Baptist." Not a bad compliment for a nutcase.

I wonder how many people are stuck in lives that offer them no meaning, no purpose, and no significance. And they are Christians. And they know that thing they were created to do. But they don't do it.

God calls and they ignore the call. They turn the other way. They allow fear, lack of faith, and an absence of courage to win the day. Again. And time marches on and the call from God grows fainter and the emptiness grows stronger.

In the depths of their soul, they know they are supposed to reach the inner-city, take the gospel to a foreign land, help the poor, start that ministry, proclaim the story of Jesus . . . They know. They know, they know, they know.

At some point we have to realize that our lives are a vapor. We're not cats. We don't get 9 lives. We have one shot at this thing called life and there are no do-overs. Either we're going to go for it, launch out on the Great Adventure of Faith and fulfill God's plan for our lives or we're going to settle. For less. For less than what God had planned for us.

So how 'bout it? Tired of the same 'ole same 'ole? Tired of just getting by? Tired of saying no to God? Still longing for that which will give your life the meaning and purpose and direction your heart desires?

Then do something about it! Take a first step. Talk to someone. Share your heart. Share those dreams God planted in your heart long ago. Don't worry that they might think you're crazy. It's not their dream. Just tell someone.

Then take some more steps. Plan. Think. Pray. Read the Word. Read it again. Listen as He speaks. Count the cost.

Then quit it. That safe life. Those negative relationships. That job. That career. That comfort zone you've lived in for so long. And begin to live. Really live. Live for the glory of God and the benefit of others. And through hard times and good times and confusing times and marvelous times watch as the Great God of the Universe uses you to make a difference in this life and the one to come.

So get going. Time's a wastin'!

It all starts the same way. All of it. All great movements, innovations, products, organizations. They all start the same way. With an idea.

Someone thinks it. Someone dreams it. Someone wonders if it could be.

And that someone might be you. You have an idea that could make a difference. You have an idea that could change lives. So you think some more and you dream some more and the idea takes root and it won't let go. It hangs around and goes deeper and grips your heart. You think about it and think about it and think about it. And you smile. Because you know. You know that if it happens, it will be great. It will be amazing. You can see it. You can feel it. You just know.

And then one day, the essential ingredient is added to the mix. Belief. One day you believe it will happen. With all your heart and all your soul, you believe.

The team will win. The business will start. The product will be made. You believe. The diploma will be earned. The organization will be formed. The building will be built. You believe. The service will be provided. The money will be raised. The cure will be found. You believe.

And you have to believe. You have to believe it will happen. That hard work and persistence and prayer and more hard work will all, somehow, someway, come together at the right time and against all the odds and all the naysayers and all the impossibilities and it will happen. It just will. You believe.

And if you don't believe? It will never happen. It will remain an idea. A good idea, but only an idea. And nothing will change and nobody will be blessed and everything will stay the same.

But on that day when you believe, when you really, really, really believe, then you come alive. Then you take action. And things start to happen. And resources appear and people appear and the idea begins to form into reality. And it's amazing.

So what about you? Do you have an idea? Do you believe?

Has it ever happened to you? Even once? If it had, you would know it. You would recall it. You would never forget.

It happened to her. It happened this week when she returned to Haiti after being in the States for a few weeks. Her name is Rachel. She's tiny. She's young. She has few resources. But she has a heart the size of Dallas. What happened? As she returned to Haiti to start our In-Patient Malnutrition Program for starving children, something so profound happened that she can't let it go. She won't let it go. It has solidified a calling in her heart. According to her, this is what happened:

"If there was ever a doubt in my mind about why I am still in Haiti after 2 years, it was shattered this afternoon. Today a little boy died of malnutrition. He was 9 months old. The rest of the world will go on as normal, but his Mama won't forget. I refuse to forget. I refuse to let him be another statistic with no name or face. His name was Elison. And in his memory and for every child that comes after him, I will fight. No child should ever starve to death. It's an evil in this world that I will never understand. Elison's battle here on earth may have been lost, but his victory is in the arms of Jesus."

"I will fight." That's what she said. You see, there are some things worth fighting for. There are some things worth giving everything you've got.

Has it ever happened to you? Have you found that one thing for which you were willing to fight? That one thing that stirred your heart and your mind so much that you were willing to sacrifice and give and go and do whatever needed to be done?

Have you ever felt your soul come alive in such a way that you knew you were here for a reason? You knew your life had a purpose and you were going to fulfill that purpose no matter the cost. Has it ever happened to you?

There's nothing like it. There's nothing like devoting this one life here on Earth to something that matters, to something that makes a difference, to something you just can't let go.

It happened to Rachel. Has it happened to you?

What's it like? What's it like when you know? When you know it's almost over.

What's it like when you get the diagnosis and you're given three months? What's it like when you wake up and you're no longer in your 20s, or 40s, or 60s?

Are you sad? Are you depressed? Do you cry or fight or deny?

I suppose we've always known. But when we're younger it's not real. When we're healthy it's someone else.

So what do you do? Do you reminisce? Do you look at old photo albums? Do you talk to family and friends and tell them things you always wanted to tell them?

Are you finally honest? With your spouse and your children and your friends? With yourself?

What do you do? Do you have regrets and wish you'd done more? Do you revel in accomplishments? Do you listen to sad, old, sappy songs?

Do you realize most things you desired didn't matter? That most things you worried about were unimportant? Do you have better perspective and a wiser heart? What do you do?

Do you find God? Or at least look for him? Do you think about heaven and those who've already gone? Do you look forward to seeing Him, the One you've known by faith but long to see face-to-face?

What do you do when you know? When you really, finally, completely . . . know?

In an interview, Amy Grant said that several years ago she was on her way to get on a tour bus when she went by to see her mother who had Alzheimer's disease. As she was leaving, Amy said, "I've got to go sing, mom." Her mother said, "You sing?" Amy said, "Yes. I sing and I write songs." Her mom asked about the kinds of songs she sings and if she would sing for her.

Then, as Amy was walking out the door, her mom called after her. "Hey, would you do me a favor?" Amy said, "Yes, what?" And her mom said, "When you walk out on that stage, sing something that matters."

It seems that Amy Grant's mom, though not even in her right mind, was on to something. If you're going to sing, sing something that matters. I've been thinking a lot about that statement the last few days. It has struck me that since God is right and life is a vapor, we all have a very limited amount of time on this planet. So it seems that while we're here, we might as well make it count.

If you're going to preach, preach something that matters.
If you're going to teach, teach something that matters.
If you're going to write, write something that matters.
If you're going to work, do work that matters.

How many people are just meandering aimlessly through life, wasting precious time, and doing nothing that really matters? All the while, there is a great big world out there with incredible opportunities for someone who is willing to invest the time and effort to do something that matters.

Fortunately, that doesn't mean everyone has to do something big or famous. Some things that matter are small and little-known. But they still matter. They matter to family members and to friends and even to strangers. Most of all, they matter to God.

Amy Grant's mom was right. If you're going to sing, sing something that matters.

Do you ever think about it? I know, it can be depressing. But it might be helpful to think about it. After all, it's going to happen. So we should probably give it a little thought.

I thought about it the last few days. Had to. I got a call that a dear friend died and they want me to speak at the funeral. That means I'll have to say something. About my deceased friend. I'll talk about her life, what she did, how she lived. I'll talk about the impact she made and what her life was all about. There'll be no shortage of material. Won't have to exaggerate or stretch the truth or search for something important to say. It's all there. In the record of her life.

While thinking of my friend, I realized all over again that they'll have a service for me one day. I wonder what they'll say. Because they'll have to say something. It won't be a silent funeral. Oh sure, some people say they don't care what is said at their funeral because they won't be there. But maybe we should care. After all, what they say will be a reflection of how we lived. And that matters.

What will they say at your service? Will they talk about how much you loved your family and made them a priority? That you were there for them and guided them and spent time with them? Will they discuss how you blessed the lives of many outside your family? How you helped and encouraged and taught and invested in the lives of others? That you made a difference? That people's lives were changed for the good because you lived on this earth?

Will they talk about your love for God and how you lived out His word? Will they use words like honesty and integrity, faithful and true? Will they discuss your work in His Kingdom? How you shared His love? How you told others about the cross and the empty tomb? How your life and your words were a witness to His grace?

What will they say? Maybe we should give it a little thought. It will be here before we know it. And someone will be asked to stand and speak. About you. About me. What will they say?

She was an angel. Straight from heaven. Or so it seemed.

Earlier this week, I had lunch with a very nice man I had briefly met only days before. As we sat in the restaurant, I asked about his family and his work. A year earlier, he had left his job of 15 years to pursue other work, ministry-related work.

This past year had been difficult. His mother became ill and he looked after her until she died. Then his teenage daughter was diagnosed with a brain tumor and had surgery. She's doing better now. The serious illnesses of his two family members kept him from fully pursuing his next line of work. I said to him that this past year must have been very difficult. He didn't complain, mind you. He just responded, described some of the difficulties, and said it was a challenging year. Now he's ready to move forward, excited about the future.

And that's when she appeared. I had seen her when we sat down. She was directly across from us at another table and she was dining alone. Apparently she had been eavesdropping, quietly listening to our conversation.

She stood, walked a few steps to our table, and placed five twenty dollar bills near the plate of my new friend. As she walked away she said, "Use this as you need it."

I had never seen this woman. Neither had my friend. As she walked out the door, I jumped from my seat and followed her, my friend close behind. We finally caught up with her and asked her why she had left the money. She simply said to use the money as needed. And then she was gone.

We went back inside and sat down. Not a word was said as we contemplated what had just happened. Tears formed in my friend's eyes. It had been a long year.

You see, He sent her. He sent her to that restaurant on that day to hear that conversation. He touched her heart and she responded. And my new friend was blessed.

She was an angel. Straight from heaven. Or so it seemed.

Stan Buckley

Is it possible? Can it be done? Can you live a life of meaning and significance without living for something bigger than yourself? Is it enough just to meander through life, try to make ends meet, gather a few toys along the way, grow old, and die?

Is it enough for me to be successful in my work, make good money, and provide well for my immediate family? Is it enough to focus on me and mine and not much else?

It seems that life takes on greater meaning when we find something that is beyond ourselves, that makes a difference in the lives of others. Something that brings good and God and hope into the world of otherwise hopeless people.

The few times I have ventured beyond myself, looked to something more than myself, I have found incredible joy. There has been that hard-to-describe sense of purpose and satisfaction that simply being successful cannot provide.

So what is it for you? What grabs your heart and won't let go? What is that thing, that cause, that work that makes you smile, that drives you to do more and tell others and sacrifice greater? What is it that makes such a difference in the lives of others that it makes a difference in your life? Do that. Do it more and better. Do it today. Experience the joy and satisfaction of that something that is bigger than you. Do that.

I'm proud of it. Really, really, proud of it. I shouldn't be so proud because it's not that big of a deal. But I'm proud.

Two days ago, we were told that the hike up the mountain in eastern Haiti would take four hours, and there, we would see the leaks in the little pipe that brings water from the spring to the people in the village below. After four hours, we would see the leaky pipe, but we wouldn't see the spring that feeds the pipe. It was another two hours.

So we started walking. It was beautiful and stunning and breathtaking. The higher we got, the better the view. And it was cool. The perfect temperature to climb a mountain.

We completed the four hour climb in less than four hours. That's because we are great mountain climbers. And explorers. Like Lewis and Clark.

We ate our sack lunches and we sat and we talked and we admired the view. And then we had to decide. Do we take what we had accomplished and go back down the mountain or do we continue up the mountain to the spring that is the source of life for countless Haitians? Do we go all the way?

I didn't want to go. It had been a good experience. I was happy and content. I wasn't tired or sore. We could go back down the mountain, reunite with the rest of our team that was at the little one-room church pulling teeth and caring for sick people, and everything would be fine. Perfectly fine.

Then I had to ask myself WWLD. What would Lee do? What would my friend who was pulling teeth in the little church do if he were in my shoes? Would he hike to the spring or would he turn around and walk back? I didn't have to think long. I knew what Lee would do. Lee would go. He would go all the way to the top of the mountain. He would complete the journey holding nothing back and leaving no challenge unmet. Because that's what Lee does. That's how he lives his life. And he rarely goes alone. He takes someone with him. Usually lots of someones. And he encourages and inspires and tells everyone they can do it because he believes they can. And because he believes they can, they believe they can.

So we left. Going higher. Much higher. And the path became more narrow and more steep and more challenging and more beautiful until we arrived at the spring, the source of water for the valley below. Then we rested.

After a long while, we started back. Then the strangest thing happened. Whenever I walked uphill or on flat ground, I felt nothing. No pain. No strain. Nothing. But whenever I walked downhill, someone stabbed my left knee with a steak knife. Every. Single. Downhill. Step. And, as it turns out, walking from the top of the mountain to the bottom of the mountain was mostly downhill.

The last two hours were miserable. Extremely painful. Didn't think I could keep going. But I did. Nine hours after we began our climb that morning, we completed the hike. And even though I am currently crippled, barely able to walk, I'm glad we did it. Glad we kept going. Glad we made it to the top of that mountain.

I don't know why I'm so glad we did it. Don't know why I'm so proud of our hike to the top of the mountain. But I am. I'm really glad. And really proud.

But most of all, I'm proud to have a friend named Lee.

It doesn't do any good. It never helps. In fact, it's defeating and debilitating and depressing. So why do I do it? Why do I play the comparison game?

I can always find someone who is taller or richer or smarter. I can always find someone with a nicer car or a bigger house or a better resume. I can always find someone who is more handsome or more educated or more something. Always.

Even in the helping world, I can always find someone with a bigger ministry or a better ministry or a more effective ministry. In Haiti, there are lots of groups doing great work. Some have been established for decades. Some have huge budgets and nice facilities and large staffs. Some are reaching large numbers of people. They're doing a better job. Or at least it seems that way.

But when I stop comparing, I realize He didn't call me to be them. He didn't call me to do their ministry. He didn't call me to try and be like them. He created me to be me. He called me to do my work. He called me to be like Jesus.

After all, He said that I am fearfully and wonderfully made. After all, He sent His Son to die for me. And just like the 1 sheep out of the 99, if I had been the only one lost, He still would have sent the Son to rescue me and bear my burden on that old rugged cross.

So today, I think I'll just thank Him for creating me to be me. I think I'll just strive to be the best me possible. And I'll thank Him for the work He has given me to do, and I'll try to do it the best way I can do it. And that will be enough. More than enough.

Why not? Why not you? Oh, I know. You're not smart enough, or pretty enough, or wealthy enough. You don't have the right degree or the right friends or the right . . . something. And that past. Oh, that past. If people only knew. No, it can't be you.

But if you had all these things, you could be the one. You could get it done. And you'd be glad to. If you had all these things and if you were all these things, you could feed the hungry, befriend the lonely, or comfort the hurting. You could love the unlovely and forgive the guilty. You could share His love and spread His word and teach His plan. But you don't have all these things. You're not all these things. So God can't use you. He would probably like to, but He just can't.

After all, only the really smart people and the really beautiful people and the really rich people can feed the hungry and comfort the hurting and visit the imprisoned. Only the perfect people can take care of the widows and the orphans. Only the flawless people can share His love and encourage the downtrodden and embrace the suffering.

Well, except for Abraham. And Moses. And Rahab and David and Peter and Timothy and Paul. They were liars and killers and prostitutes and adulterers and traitors and nobodies and murderers.

And except for Rick and Tony and John and Mallory and Cathy and Dale and Diana. And, of course, Sam and Melanie and Wayne and Jill and June and James. All not-so-famous friends of mine who are doing amazing things in the name of our amazing God. Somewhere along the way, they stopped making excuses and decided to be obedient. No matter the cost. No matter the obstacles. No matter their insecurities or inabilities. They just said yes to God.

You see, it really wasn't about them. It wasn't about their skills or their looks or their bank accounts. It was about Him. It was about His plan and His strength and His wisdom.

So we ask. Why not? Why not you?

What will they say? They'll say something. You can count on that. But what will it be? You know, when you're gone. When your time is up, when you're called home, when you're no longer with us.

Will they say you were nice or athletic or smart? Will they talk about your family or your cooking or your many accomplishments? What will they say?

I was reading this morning about a lady named Tabitha. She died. Happens to the best of us. But this guy named Peter went to her house. He prayed for her and told her to get up. And she did. Pretty cool.

But, as incredible as that was, it's not the most significant part of the story. After all, she died again later. The most significant part of the story took place when the writer of the story (some guy named Luke) gave a brief description of Tabitha. He wrote that she was "always doing good and helping the poor." That's how he described her. Not that she was beautiful or smart or funny, though I kinda like beautiful, smart, funny people.

Luke wanted us to know this lady was special, that she was to be admired. Why? Because she spent her time doing good stuff and helping poor people. He didn't say that she WASN'T beautiful or smart or funny. She may have been. But if she were ONLY beautiful and smart and funny and she never did good and rarely helped the poor, then her beauty and her brains and her sense of humor would not have amounted to much.

It's true. They're going to say something. Maybe not for long. Maybe not a lot of them. But somebody, somewhere is going to say something. About you. About me. What will they say?

It's going to happen. And there's nothing we can do about it. One day, whether we're expecting it or not, it will happen. Many will be sad. A few may be glad. But in the end, it doesn't matter. It's going to happen.

We can postpone it. At least for a little while. We can ignore it, until we just can't. We can pretend it won't happen, but it will. It's going to happen.

And deep down, we know it's going to happen. Because it always does. It never fails to happen.

I have often wondered what it will be like. You know, that day when death takes me away. Takes me from this life to the next. I don't think I'm afraid. But I'm very interested in what will happen. Kind of excited, even. I think it will be wonderful. The ultimate freedom. All those things that bind us and hurt us and distress us. They'll be gone. He won't let them be there.

On that day, I want to see J.C. and Ruby, Prentiss and Lois. They were really good grandparents. And I want to see Horace, the grandfather I never knew who died in Germany at the end of the war. I really want to meet him. He's kind of a hero of mine. I've lived a fantastic life thus far, thanks to him and his buddies.

More than anything, I want to see Him. I just want to see Him. I want to see His face and His hands and His feet. And I want to tell Him how much I love Him and how sorry I am for the times I disappointed Him and how thankful I am for everything – all the many, many things - He has done for me. I want to thank Him for the cross and I want to tell Him I didn't deserve that kind of sacrifice but I'm awfully glad He did it. I want to tell Him that. I want Him to know how thankful I am. I just want Him to know.

It's going to happen. And I can't wait to see Him.

According to them, she didn't matter. She was racially and morally inferior. And she was a she. It was all her fault. Well, most of it. Maybe not the racial thing or the female thing. Those weren't her fault but they were bad anyway. And somebody had to be blamed.

But the moral thing, that was definitely her. She made those choices. She slept with all those men. Nobody forced her. She did it because she was bad. And immoral. Nasty, really. And it didn't matter that some of them wanted to sleep with her too. They wondered, imagined, what it would be like. But that didn't matter. She had done it. She was bad.

And now, as a result of her badness, and her she-ness, and her mixed race-ness, she would spend the rest of her life on the outside. Shunned. Ignored. And there was nothing she could do about it. Nothing.

And then He appeared. He walked right up to her and started talking, like she was a real person. He knew all about her. He knew she was a she. He knew she was of mixed race. And he knew she had had five husbands and was now shacking up with another man. He knew it all. And he talked to her anyway.

She was stunned. She knew it was not normal for a man of a so-called pure race, who was seemingly righteous, to talk to someone like her. He seemed to care about her and not so much about social norms. He just treated her with kindness and dignity, something she hadn't experienced in a long time, if ever.

So she told the other people in her community about Him. They invited Him to stay a while longer. And He did. And she was changed. And they were changed. They found a peace and a joy and a hope they had never known.

I wonder how many more are out there. How many more bad people are out there wishing someone would talk to them like a normal person? How many more are on the outside wondering what it would be like to be on the inside? How many more are just people trying to make it but don't know where to turn?

And why don't I do like He did?

I get it, I get it, I get. I really do. Been to seminary. Have the degrees. Pastored for years. Understand the theology. I know that works will never save me. I get it. I know I am a rotten sinner saved only by grace through faith and not by works. I know it, I understand it, and I believe it.

But that's not the end of the discussion. At least according to Jesus. He once said that He's going to come again, "and then He will reward each person according to what He has done." Another time, He said that not everyone is going to enter His Kingdom, "but only he who does the will of My Father." Still another time He said that His followers are the ones who give food to the hungry, water to the thirsty, hospitality to the stranger, clothes to the naked, help to the sick, and a visit to the imprisoned. He also said, when comparing followers to trees, that His followers would be recognized by their fruit.

You can do your own research, read your own commentaries, and try to determine what role works play in our faith. We can debate that role. We can discuss that role. We can disagree on the exact role that works play in the Christian life. But we can all agree that works play some role in our Christian life.

In other words, it matters how we live. It's not enough to say a magic prayer or employ Easy Believism or get the Fire Insurance Policy and then live our lives as though we have never encountered the Risen Lord. If that's what we believe, or, more importantly, if that's how we live, then I am afraid many of us will hear those awful words one day: "I never knew you. Away from Me."

So, while there is time, while we have ample opportunities, while it is still day, let us spur one another on to good deeds. Let us love one another, serve one another, pour blessings onto one another. Let us sacrifice time and talent and treasure for the least of these. Let us die to self, do without, and make much of Jesus and the ones He seemed to take so much time with—the poor and the sick and the sinful and the outcasts.

We have much to do. Let's get busy.

Stan Buckley

Shut up. Just shut up. Stop talking so much. It's annoying and it's harmful and it's certainly not helpful. So shut up.

OK, I'm sorry. I know you're not supposed to say shut up. We teach our children that's not a nice thing to say. And it's not.

But the truth is, sometimes that's what we need to do. Keep our mouths closed. Keep our thoughts to ourselves. We need to stop talking.

I'm sure it's not original with him, but my dad always said, "It's better to remain silent and be thought a fool than to speak up and remove all doubt."

And there was this other guy who was supposed to be pretty smart. His father named him Solomon and he wrote a lot of wise sayings. This morning I read some of his sayings in Proverbs 10. I read chapter 10 because today is the 10th day of the month and I always read a chapter in Proverbs that corresponds with the day of the month. That way I never have to wonder what I should be reading or where I left off.

Anyway, today Solomon said to shut up. Over and over, he warned about the trouble we get ourselves in when we keep on talking. He said, "A chattering fool comes to ruin" and "violence overwhelms the mouth of the wicked." He said, "The mouth of a fool invites ruin," and "whoever spreads slander is a fool."

He also said, "When words are many, sin is not absent, but he who holds his tongue is wise." He counseled that "the lips of the righteous nourish many" and "the mouth of the righteous brings forth wisdom, but a perverse tongue will be cut out." He wrote, "Reckless words pierce like a sword, but the tongue of the wise brings healing." The last verse of chapter 10 says, "The lips of the righteous know what is fitting, but the mouth of the wicked only what is perverse."

This is good advice but not easy to do. Especially if you like to talk. Especially if, like me, you have made a living talking.

But it seems we can learn a lot if we remain silent and listen. We can learn about others. About their trials and hurts and difficulties. And by simply listening, we can ease their pain and share their burdens.

It's not nice to say, but sometimes we just need to shut up.

Big. And Strong. Famous and wealthy. Loud and confident and powerful and rich. These are the things we admire. These are the things, and the ways, we teach our children. If we are not these things, we long to be.

But that's not what He said. Strangely, He said that whoever humbles himself is the greatest. Notice He didn't say that whoever humbles himself is being a nice guy, or is doing something neat, or is a pretty good fellow. No. Whoever humbles himself is the greatest. The best. Top of the line. He has ascended to the highest place. That's what He said.

And He didn't just say it, He lived it out. This Jesus, this God-in-the-flesh, not only talked about humbling Himself, but He actually humbled Himself. Don't you like it when someone is real? And genuine? And lives out what he says he believes? Makes a person so much more believable. Especially someone with the resume of this guy. Education: knows everything. Work Experience: created the world, healed blind people and deaf people and paralyzed people, raised the dead to life. Career Objective: save the world.

This guy with this resume humbled Himself to hang out with the lowest of the low. Spent time with them and took a genuine interest in them. And then there was that time He took the basin and water and washed the feet of His closest friends, doing a job they wouldn't do. He even washed the feet of one of the guys who, later that evening, would betray Him. He knew it was going to happen and He washed the guy's feet anyway. Then there was the ultimate example of humbling Himself when He allowed Himself to be ridiculed and tortured and killed. All for the sake of others.

Maybe, just maybe, we could follow his lead to greatness and humble ourselves. Maybe we could cease striving to make sure we're noticed and acknowledged and rewarded. Maybe we could just serve other people, invest in their lives, watch them grow and blossom, and become the people God wants them to be. Maybe we could help and bless and never look for credit. And then maybe we really will be great—in His eyes.

Whoever humbles himself is the greatest.

Would love to have been there. Talk about a Who's Who gathering. It was the Mt. Rushmore of first century believers: Peter, James, John, Paul. In one room at one time. Doesn't get any better.

It would be like a gathering with Michelangelo, Raphael, Rembrandt, and da Vinci. It would be like George Washington, Thomas Jefferson, Abraham Lincoln, and Teddy Roosevelt all together at once. For sports fans, it would be like Joe Montana, Roger Staubach, Terry Bradshaw, and Johnny Unitas in one room and Babe Ruth, Joe DiMaggio, Ted Williams, and Willie Mays in another room. It would be like all of these combined. Except better. Infinitely better.

It seems those four giants of the faith would have much to discuss, much to consider. A vast wealth of history and experience and faithfulness were at their disposal. So at the end of a fruitful meeting, what was the last thing discussed? What was the one thing they wanted to emphasize as they parted ways? Must have been important. Must have mattered. Must have taken top priority.

Was it Calvinism v. Arminianism? Or contemporary music v. traditional music? Or the placement of the offering during the worship service or who's on which committee? Shockingly, those items weren't even mentioned. So what was it? What was so important it had to be discussed before they parted ways?

Remember the poor.

Surely that was not it. I think they meant to say remember the buildings, remember the budget, remember the programs. They must have misspoken. Or maybe it was written down wrongly. They probably said remember the length of the service or remember to put your name in the bulletin to get full credit.

Remember the poor? Yes, that was it. Look it up. Galatians 2:10. Remember the poor, the hungry, the thirsty, the homeless. Remember the widows and the orphans, those with no voice and no clout and no one to speak on their behalf. Remember the defenseless and the harassed, the persecuted and the oppressed. Remember the hurting and the suffering and the lonely.

Remember the poor. In His name, and just as He did, remember the poor.

It was a little strange. Everywhere we went, we heard languages we did not understand. In the elevator, on the sidewalk, in the subway. Everywhere. Rarely did we hear English, especially English as we speak it. Instead, we heard what we believe was Spanish. And French. And Chinese. And Japanese. And many more.

We were in New York City that week, my daughter and I. She was moving off to college the following week so we took a last minute father-daughter trip. It was nice. Just the two of us seeing the sights and enjoying time together. Statue of Liberty, 911 Memorial, Empire State Building, Chinatown, Central Park, Rockefeller Center, St. Patrick's, Broadway plays. And shopping. Lots of shopping. It was fun being with her in that amazing city.

I was reminded during that week that God is not an English-speaking God. None of the early God-followers spoke English. Not Adam or Noah. Not Abraham or Isaac or Jacob. Moses and Joshua and David didn't think, write, or read English. Isaiah, Jeremiah, and Nehemiah? Not a word of English.

In fact, when this Christianity thing started, no one involved spoke English. Not Peter. Not James or John. Not Paul or Timothy or Barnabas. No one. They lived their entire lives and never heard one word of English.

And the One we worship and follow and love? The One whose praises we sing? The One who suffered and bled and died for us? Nope. Not a word. Not one word of English.

It's a bit unnerving to consider this lack of English in the biblical record. After all, English is the only language I speak, and it's the language through which I came to know God and His Word and His Son. I'm afraid I have subconsciously assumed God was an English-speaking God. Or at least He liked English the best and spoke it the most.

But maybe that's not true. Maybe He doesn't have a favorite language. At least I hope not. Because if He did, it would likely be Hebrew. Or Greek or Arabic. And I'm not too good with any of those.

While walking through Times Square with my daughter and hearing every language but English, I thought about that verse. That verse in Revelation that describes the scene in the throne room of heaven in which those surrounding Jesus sang,

> "You are worthy to take the scroll and to open its seals,
> Because you were slain,
> And with your blood you purchased men for God
> From every tribe and language and people and nation."

They'll all be there one day. Every tribe. Every people. Every nation. And yes, every language. Including English. And instead of fighting one another and hating one another and being suspicious of one another, we'll love one another. And worship together. And finally realize that our God is a lot bigger and a lot greater than any one language. And that will be nice. Really nice.

Worthless. Pointless. A big fat waste of time. That's what your religion is. That's what your faith is. All that going to church, attending Sunday School, serving on that committee. Worthless. Might as well go fishing, take up knitting, find something else to do.

How do I know? It's what the Bible says. James, the half-brother of Jesus, wrote that our religion is worthless if we don't keep a tight rein on our tongues. So all that gossiping and talking about people and lying and slandering and stirring up trouble, it comes with a price. It has consequences. And perhaps the biggest consequence is that it renders our faith worthless. Not simply ineffective. Not merely deficient. Worthless. Worth nothing.

You can argue otherwise. You can say it doesn't really render your faith worthless. You can say that's just hyperbole, exaggeration. But you're wrong.

If you don't keep a tight rein on your tongue, your religion is worthless. Reminds me of the Proverb I read this morning: "Even a fool is thought wise if he keeps silent." Maybe today would be a good day for us to practice keeping our ears open and our mouths shut.

It never works. I keep trying, but it never works. I should probably give up on it, but for some reason I don't. I keep trying and trying and trying. I try even though it's futile and even though it exhausts me.

I'm not alone. There are many others who also try. And there are countless ones who have tried before us. You'd think we would learn. But we don't.

We press on, seeking to have our thirsty souls satisfied. And they are thirsty. Our souls long for meaning, purpose, and contentment. Our souls, the essence of who we are, long for satisfaction and fulfillment.

So we search. We chase after academic achievement or career success. We look to money or fame. We travel, we acquire. We seek new experiences and new people. And yet we are still thirsty. Sometimes we look in dark places. We drink from dirty pools. As stated in the ancient book of Jeremiah, "They have forsaken me, the spring of living water, and have dug their own cisterns, broken cisterns that cannot hold water." Eventually, we face the consequences of our wayward actions.

And yet the answer has been there all along. He gave us the answer when He said, "If anyone is thirsty, let him come to me and drink." It is in Him, the living and resurrected Christ, that our souls find rest. It is in Him, and with Him, and through Him, that our deep longings are finally satisfied. We follow Him as He leads us beside the still waters where we drink the pure, clean water of hope and redemption and we are finally refreshed and made whole.

I have sought to satisfy my thirsty soul in those things that cannot satisfy. It never works. I have also drunk from the deep waters of Jesus. I have found His claims to be true. I know He satisfies. I know that in Him my thirst is quenched and my soul is at rest.

I was hungry and you discussed the latest cool book about whether it's really good to help people.

I was thirsty and you spent all your time blaming the poor for being poor.

I was a stranger and you griped about how those people going on mission trips are doing it all wrong.

I needed clothes and you debated whether it does any good to meet physical needs because people are going to die and go to hell so all we need to do is give them a booklet about how to be saved and stop wasting time trying to temporarily help people. You said that as you ate lunch at the fancy restaurant and then drove away in your new car on your way to your big house.

I was sick and you complained that you have lots of people around you that need help so why should we help those people over there. You said that while you weren't helping people here or there.

I was in prison and you talked about how people should be locked away forever and forgotten.

There we were. Just the two of us. Riding down I-20 somewhere in Scott County, Mississippi on a Sunday morning headed to church. A Haitian and an American.

As we sang, just the two of us, I glanced over and saw his hand raised. Together, we were praising our God, singing His praises.

I thought about his village and his church and how they are so different from my town and my church. Then a tear rolled down my cheek as I thought of how the love of Christ had bridged that huge gap, had made us friends for over two years, brothers in Christ, and co-laborers in the gospel.

I had wanted him to hear some of my favorite songs so I plugged my iPhone into the car stereo and hit play. To make sure he understood the words, I called up the lyrics on my iPad. So we sang. Together and not very well.

O the blood
Crimson love
Price of life's demand
Shameful sin
Placed on Him
The hope of every man

O the blood of Jesus washes me
O the blood of Jesus shed for me
What a sacrifice that saved my life
Yes, the blood, it is my victory

We sang about His love and His deeds and His sacrifice. We joined Carrie Underwood and sang How Great Thou Art. We just sang.

Later we would talk. For hours we talked as we drove to another church and then home at night. We would talk about differences and poverty and money and opportunity and hope and the future. We would talk about his family and my family. But earlier, in the car, on the way to church, we just sang of the One who had brought us together and made such a difference in our lives.

He's not looking. Not paying attention. Completely uninterested.

I was reading about this guy named David who became a king. A real live king. Crown and everything. The day he was chosen to be king, God made an interesting statement. A statement that goes against the way we think and act and live. God said, "Man looks at the outward appearance, but the Lord looks at the heart."

I thought about that and then I thought about us. We are strange creatures. We spend a lot of time and a lot of effort and a lot of money on the outward appearance. The right clothes and the right shoes and the right car and the right this and the right that. Lots of time. Lots of effort. Lots of money.

And after we've spent all that time and all that effort and all that money, God says, "You look great. You look sharp. You look distinguished. But I don't care."

That's right. He doesn't care. He's not interested. He's not even looking. So it seems awfully strange that we spend all that time and all that effort and all that money and God's not even looking.

I don't think it means we have to dress like a slob and fail to take care of ourselves. That would be bad too.

But it seems that if God is not even looking at our outward appearance, then we might spend less time and less effort and less money there and we might focus more on the heart. Who we really are. Our character. Our convictions. Our thoughts and motivations. That's where He's looking. That's what He's interested in. That's what really matters.

The outward appearance? He's not even looking.

It's marvelous. And wonderful. And fantastic. It's encouraging and inspiring and challenging.

It's also big and complex and confusing. It's hard to understand and difficult to explain. There are 66 books with 40 authors. There's history and poetry and prophecy and law. How do you get your arms around something as big and varied as the Bible? Where do you start? How do you read it?

Here's an idea, something I've done for years. Take a book of the Bible. Take Philippians. It's in the New Testament and it's only four chapters. Read all four chapters. At one sitting. That's right. Read the entire book. It's not that big. In fact, in my Bible it's only three pages. I timed it this morning. Took me 6 minutes to read it. Six whole minutes!

So, on day one, read the entire book. Do it again on days two, three, four and five. Here's what will happen. On day four, the light bulb will come on. You'll begin to see things you've never seen before. You'll see details you've missed. You'll receive fresh insight and new thoughts.

Why? Because it was designed to be read that way. We call it a book, but it's really a letter. It's a letter from a guy named Paul to a bunch of Christians in the city of Philippi (northeast Greece). Suppose I received a three page letter from you, opened it, read the first paragraph on the first page, then folded the letter and put it back in the envelope. I would have no idea what you were trying to communicate. I would need to read the entire letter. At one sitting. Then I would have a much better understanding of what you were trying to tell me. It's the same with Paul's letter.

Also, if you read the entire book of Philippians every day, by the time day four rolls around, you'll understand the overall theme of the letter. You'll know what Paul was trying to communicate. You'll be familiar with the flow of the letter. Then, the details will begin to emerge. It's a simple truth that the more you look at something, the more things you'll see. For example, if you briefly glance at a painting, you might realize what is being portrayed. If you walk away immediately, you'll recall only one or two things about the painting. But if you stop and study it for a while and come back several days in a row, you'll see colors and lines and details that you didn't see the first time you looked at it. It's the same with Paul's letter.

So, read Philippians. All of it. Every day. It's fascinating and fun and challenging and insightful. It's one of my favorite books in all the Bible. Ultimately, it's about joy. Joy in the good times and joy in the bad times. And I don't know about you, but I could use a little more joy.

Stop it. Just stop it. All the whining. All the complaining. All the protecting of self interests. Just stop it. All the parading. All the preserving of buildings and paintings and pews and other objects. All the frantic, angry, ridiculous protection of programs and ministries that stopped working years ago. It's not who He is. It's not what He is about. So stop it. Just stop it, Christian.

Our country is going to hades in the proverbial hand basket, fewer people are interested in the things of God, church attendance has declined dramatically, more people are leaving the church, and our biggest concern is that our Sunday School room was 2 degrees too warm. And we are angry about it. Truly angry. Lashing out and acting ugly. Over 2 degrees in our Sunday School room.

People are unemployed, the lost are going to hell, children are starving, diseases are destroying entire people groups, women walk 5 hours each way to get clean water. Every day. But we don't care one bit about that. We're angry about our Sunday School room. We're angry, really angry, because we didn't like one of the songs that was sung in the worship service or that the preacher went an extra 5 minutes.

Who are we? What have we become? We look nothing like our Jesus. He would recognize little of what we do. In fact, if He were here today, many of us who call ourselves Christians would hate Him and ridicule Him and refuse to listen to Him. We would say He is out of touch or He's gone off the deep end or He just doesn't understand. He's crazy.

After all, this is the guy who hung out with poor people and sick people and desperate people. He mingled with prostitutes and the worst kind of sinners. We don't even know people like that, much less hang out with them.

He was revolutionary. What He said was different. His approach to life was countercultural. And yet we have mainstreamed Him. Tamed Him. All for our own purposes. All for our own interests. All for us.

And yet, this is the guy who said: sell everything you have and give to the poor, love your enemies, turn the other cheek, go the second mile, travel the narrow road, do not judge, you can't serve God and money, do not worry, repent or perish, pray for those who persecute you, carry your cross, count the cost, blessed are you when people insult you because of me, it's easier for a camel to go through the eye of a needle than a rich man to enter heaven, and when you give a luncheon, invite the poor, the crippled, the lame, the blind.

Who's doing all that? Or any of it? One leader of a mainline denomination recently wrote:

"Too many contemporary clergy limit themselves to ministries of congregational care-giving – soothing the fears of the anxiously affluent. One of my pastors led a self-study of his congregation. Eighty percent responded that their chief expectation of their pastor was, 'Care for me and my family.'"

"Oblivious to our current crisis, seminaries continue to produce pastors for congregational care-giving and institutional preservation. The result is another generation of pastors who know only how to be chaplains for the status quo and managers of decline rather than leaders of a movement in transformational faith."

When do we wake up? When do we set aside pettiness and foolishness and irrelevancy? Where are those willing to be bold and different and biblical? Where are those willing to risk it all for His glory and the benefit of others? Where are those who love HIM more than their own comfort or their own desires or their own interests? Where are they?

I know you do. You miss him. You miss her. Some time ago, the great enemy Death stole your loved one. Weeks ago, months ago, perhaps years ago that grandparent, that parent, that spouse, that child was taken from you. That brother, that sister, that dear friend is no longer here with you.

And it hurts. It stings. Even after all this time, the pain is still there. The sorrow, though maybe not as intense, never fully goes away. And more than anything, you want to see him again. You want to talk with her again. You want to take a walk, share a meal, tell a story. You want to spend time with that one you loved.

I read it this morning. Surely I had read it many times before, but it was as though I was reading it for the first time. He was talking with a group of people who did not believe the dead will rise.

He said, "Now about the dead rising – have you not read in the book of Moses, in the account of the bush, how God said to him, 'I am the God of Abraham, the God of Isaac, and the God of Jacob'? He is not the God of the dead, but of the living."

By the time of Moses, Abraham and Isaac and Jacob had been dead for centuries. Yet, He was still their God. How? Because He's not the God of dead people. He's not the God of people who live for a short time and then cease to exist. He's the God of the living! He's the God of people who have eternal souls, who live forever. He's the God of people who, "even though they die, yet shall they live."

He's the God of the great Dwight L. Moody who once told a large audience, "One day you will open the paper and read that Dwight L. Moody is dead. Don't you believe it. For on that day, I will be more alive than I have ever been!"

I know you do. You miss him. You miss her. But do not despair, for on that Great Reunion Day, you will see them again.

So what? So what that you weren't the smartest in your class. Or the most popular. So what that you don't have a zillion dollars in the bank. So what that there are people who are more educated or better looking or have better connections. Are those the things God is looking for?

That doesn't seem to be what set those guys apart on that day long ago. Yet everyone could see it. It was as plain as day. They had courage. They stood tall. They were neither afraid nor ashamed. And the changed lives, who could deny?

It would make more sense if they had been highly educated. A college degree, perhaps a Master's, would have given them a leg up. Some special skill would have set them apart. But no. They were unschooled and ordinary. Not much education. Nothing special about them.

And yet, there they were. Teaching and preaching and drawing large crowds. And then there was the miracle where that crippled man stood up and started running around. No one could deny that. But how could those two guys do it? They were unschooled. And ordinary. They were just two regular Joes. Or one regular Peter and one regular John. Yep, Peter and John. Unschooled and ordinary.

So how did they do it? Was it their lack of education or their plain lives? Not exactly. Turns out there was one other thing. And those around them noticed. In fact, other people "took note that these men had been with Jesus."

That's it. That's the difference. That's what set them apart and gave them the courage and the strength to do amazing things that would make a huge difference in this world. They had been with Jesus. Spent time with Him. Listened. Loved. Obeyed. They had experienced His grace and His love and His power. They had known His peace and His joy. They had been with Jesus and it changed everything.

Unschooled and ordinary. That's who God is looking for. Ordinary folks who are willing to serve an extraordinary God. That way, when God does an amazing work, no one has to wonder who did it. God gets the credit.

People look to Him rather than us. And that's a lot better since hope and joy and peace are found in Him and not in us.

A guy named Paul once wrote, "God chose the foolish things of the world to shame the wise; God chose the weak things of the world to shame the strong. He chose the lowly things of this world and the despised things— and the things that are not—to nullify the things that are, so that no one may boast before him."

So today, if you're feeling weak and ordinary or not-so-special, you're in pretty good company. You're the one He wants to use for His glory and the benefit of others. So take heart. Be encouraged. Launch out in faith to serve Him boldly. And oh yeah, before you go, make sure you have "been with Jesus."

I need help. I need a plan. I need a way to make it easier, more simple. Because sometimes I can't remember where I left off. Sometimes I can't decide where to start.

I know I should. You know, read my Bible. I know it's good for me. I know it's God speaking to me. I've read it countless times. And I know, I really know, how good and rich and deep it is. I know how many times throughout my life God has revealed Himself and His will and His ways to me. I know how many times my life has been greatly enriched through His Word.

And I know how beautiful it is. I know about the history I love so much. I know about the poetry and the law. I recall those "aha" moments reading His Word when the profound nature of His grace has overwhelmed me until nothing else mattered. Nothing.

And yet, knowing all this, I sometimes struggle with reading the Word. The mornings are the best time for me to read, but the mornings are also when I look at my to-do list and I want to get busy. Immediately. So I can mark through some items on that list and get a jump on the day. I wake up easily and my mind goes a million miles per hour and I want to go, go, go. I want to get it all done before 8:00 a.m. Or at least a lot of it. And that's crazy, but it's what I want to do. So I do. I mark things off my list, things that were added during the night when I woke up and sent myself another email. You know, so I wouldn't forget. So I could get it done before 8:00 a.m.

Yes, I need help. I need a way. And I found it. Many years ago I found a plan and it's a plan that works. It always works. It's a plan for reading the Bible, or at least part of it.

It all has to do with the calendar. Aside from February, there are 30 or 31 days in the month. There also happen to be 31 chapters in the book of Proverbs. That makes for one chapter every day of the month. So, every day of the month you can read the chapter in Proverbs that corresponds with that day of the month. The first day of the month you read chapter 1. Today is the 21st day of the month so you read chapter 21. By the end of the month you will have read the entire book of Proverbs. By the end of the year you will have read the book of Proverbs 12 times. I have been doing this for about 18 years. That's reading through the book of Proverbs 216 times. I'm a little slow, but even I catch on after a while.

I like this plan. I never have to wonder what I should read each day. Of course, I read other parts of the Bible, but always Proverbs. And it's good. It's really good. If you want to know how to live in a way that will give you joy and keep you out of trouble, then read Proverbs. Every day. It's so practical. It was written by the wisest man who ever lived, Solomon. He wrote it to his son. It talks about everything from friends to money to women to alcohol to work ethic to how you treat the poor. It covers everything.

Yes, I need help. Lots of help. And years ago I found it. I hope you find it too.

Stan Buckley

I don't get it. I don't understand. I thought by now that I would. I thought after years of seminary training and years of pastoring and years of counseling I would understand. It would all make sense. But I still don't understand and it still doesn't make sense.

You see, it was too soon. Much too soon. He was only 51. With a wife and two kids—one in college and one in elementary school. And he died. Last Monday. There was no warning that it would happen on Monday. He had been given a clean bill of health just a few months ago. But he died. And I don't like it and I don't understand it.

You see, he was my friend and he wasn't perfect but he was good and kind and loyal. And now he's gone.

Don't misunderstand. I know we all die and I know he was a Christian and I know he is in a better place. I know all that. I believe all that. But I don't understand why he had to go now. Why he had to leave his wife and why his 9-year-old has to grow up without a father.

After all these years, I still don't understand.

I found it! It was right there all along. And it's much more simple than I imagined. I've often wondered how I can live a blessed life. Well, today I found the answer as I continued reading the words of Jesus. Here it is in Luke 11:28: "Blessed are those who hear the word of God and obey it."

That's it. Nothing more. Not a treatise. Not a four-volume historical analysis. Not overly complex. Just hear the Word of God and then do what it says.

And you know what? As I look back on over 50 years of living, I can honestly say this is true. So very true. When I do life God's way, life is good and I save myself from lots of trouble. But, when I am stubborn and sinful and do life my way and in opposition to God's word, I find myself in all kinds of trouble—marital trouble, financial trouble, personal trouble, parenting trouble, you name it.

God, who created life, has given us the best way to live this life. If we live it His way, we will be blessed. I think I'll try it!

He didn't know. He just didn't know. He was the seminary professor at my alma mater who took his own life following issues with depression and the revelation that his name was on the Ashley Madison list.

The daughter said that what broke her heart was that "he honestly doubted the fact that I would [still] love him." It broke her heart because it wasn't true. She would still love him. But he didn't know it. His shame was too great. His sorrow too strong. His embarrassment too much. So he took his own life. A life that meant so much to so many people was snuffed out in an instant. Because he didn't know.

I wonder how many are like the professor. How many think their sins are beyond love and forgiveness? How many don't know? And their lives continue in a downward spiral leading to hopelessness and defeat and, for some, a tragic ending.

But what if people knew? What if they knew they could be forgiven? What if they knew that God would forgive them and so would others? Oh, I don't mean in a way that would give license to sin but in a way that would bring redemption and forgiveness. A way that would give hope to those who are truly sorry for their sins and want to change and move forward and be clean again.

Are there people in your life who can never go beyond your love and forgiveness? Do they know that? You see, my children could never do anything that would cause me to stop loving them. I might be temporarily disappointed. I might not be happy. I might be upset. But after the initial disappointment, grace would come. Forgiveness would reign. And love would not have to return because it would have never left.

Why would I choose grace and forgiveness rather than condemnation? In part, because I know the depths of my own sinfulness. I know the depravity of my own heart. I know what I have done and what I am capable of doing. Too often I feel like the apostle Paul who wrote, "I have the desire to do what is good, but I cannot carry it out. For I do not do the good I want to do, but the evil I do not want to do – this I keep on doing." I know right from wrong but sometimes I do wrong anyway. And God still loves me, still forgives me, still wants me.

We must fight the tendency to reduce people to their worst sins and conclude nothing else about their lives matters. It's not true. It's a lie. We are more than our worst sins. We are more than our mistakes. Though sin-scarred and sin-stained, we are people created in the image of God. We are children of the King, sons and daughters of the Most High God who loves us with an everlasting love.

And we are not alone. That seminary professor was not the only Christian who had ever sinned. He was not the only believer who had ever messed up. In fact, he was just like you and just like me—a sinner saved by grace. No, he was not simply a bad man who signed up on an evil website. He was a husband and a dad and a mentor and an encourager and a friend. He was all of these things and so much more. And in spite of his sin, in spite of his mistake, he was still loved. It is our duty, our obligation, our privilege to make sure those with self-inflicted wounds know they still matter, they are still loved, and they can be forgiven.

That seminary professor who took his own life was loved by so many. But in his state of sorrow and hopelessness, he didn't know. He just didn't know.

Over and over again. Time after time. Day after day. One encounter after another. The pattern is unmistakable. People were helped. Hurts were healed. Lives were changed.

I'm only three chapters into the gospel of Mark and already He has driven out a demon, healed a lady with a fever, cured diseases, cleansed a leper, healed a paralytic, and straightened a shriveled hand. Not a bad start.

Later, He would take a bowl of water and a towel and assume the role of the lowest servant and wash the feet of His friends. He said He did so to give us an example of how we should live.

I have found in my own life that I am the most content, the most satisfied, and the most fulfilled when I am doing what He did. And I think I know why. A guy named Paul wrote a long time ago that I was created to do good works (Ephesians 2). So it only makes sense that when I am doing what I was created to do, I would experience a sense of meaning and purpose in life.

On the other hand, when my focus is on me and my success and my desires, and I fail to engage in good works, I experience a lack of contentment. My life lacks a deeper meaning and purpose. I tend to be miserable and unhappy and even angry. I suppose it makes sense that I would be unhappy when I am not doing what I was created to do.

So, I'm wondering, whose life can I invest in today? Whose life could be made better because I stopped to care and got involved? Surely there is someone. In a world filled with heartache and pain and trouble, there must be at least one person on whom I could spend some of my time and energy and love and resources. Surely there's one.

I'm thinking today that I did it again. You'd think I would learn. But I never do. I go barreling ahead and then when things aren't going perfectly or as well as I thought, I slow down, go into His presence, and confess. Confess that I haven't talked to Him much lately or sought His counsel or His strength or His power. I don't know why I do it. The result is always the same. I get worn out, frustrated, and then I go back.

Meanwhile, He's been there. Waiting. Patiently. I feel like He's saying to me, "I knew you'd come. I knew we'd be having this conversation. Again. So here I am. With all the resources in the world. Literally. If you had only asked. If you had only slowed down and spent some time with me. But you didn't. So here we are. Again."

And He welcomes me back home. Lovingly. Like the good and wise Father that He is. And I'm so grateful. Again.

I'm sick of it. Sick of it in my life. Sick of it in your life. Sick of it in the lives of most everyone I know. It's inexcusable. And ridiculous. And God hates it.

I'm sick of giving that requires no sacrifice. None. At all. We give when we can or when it's not inconvenient or after we've taken our latest vacation or bought the latest gadget. Then we'll give. And actually feel good about it. Yes, we'll feel good about giving that requires no sacrifice.

Meanwhile, people all around us are hurting and hungry and homeless and hopeless. People in other parts of the world, which are a lot closer than they used to be, won't eat tonight or won't receive medical care or won't drink clean water or won't have a decent roof over their heads. And not because they're lazy or bad or unwilling to work. They're just poor. And there are no opportunities for them to rise above their poverty. They're just poor.

And lest we get too comfortable in our no-sacrifice giving, we need to remember that He's watching. He was watching that day the widow gave her two coins. Each coin was worth a whopping one-eighth of a cent. All she had. At the same time, many rich people gave large amounts.

We would have been impressed. With the rich people. You know what He said about it? He said the little widow gave more because she gave out of her poverty. Her gift required sacrifice. He said the rich people gave out of their wealth. There was no sacrifice involved. And He wasn't impressed.

So I'm thinking that we rich people—that's most of us reading this little devotional—should stop congratulating ourselves on our no-sacrifice giving. Maybe we should stop feeling good about giving that requires nothing. Maybe then we can make a real difference in the lives of suffering people. Maybe then we can realize that God hasn't blessed us so we can sit around in a state of blessedness, but He has blessed us so we can bless others.

I hope you and I get sick. Really, really, sick. I hope we get so sick of no-sacrifice giving that we do something about it. I hope we get so incredibly sick of our no-sacrifice giving that countless lives are changed as a result. I hope we get so sick that children get to go to school, sick people get medical care, homeless people get a house, and hungry people get something to eat. That's just how sick I hope we get.

It doesn't matter what they say. It just doesn't matter. Some will like it and some will not. Some will get it and some will not. But it doesn't matter.

They didn't care. They didn't have time to care. They had stuff to do. Important stuff. Stuff that mattered. They weren't about to stop what they were doing because somebody didn't like it. Or didn't get it. Or made fun of them. They didn't care.

So that day when God filled their hearts and minds, they had to tell everybody about it. Some were amazed. Some were confused. And some made fun of them. Laughed at them. Said they were crazy. Said they were drunk.

Turns out they weren't crazy or drunk. No, they were just alive. Alive with His power and His presence. Alive with Him. And they went on to change the world. Literally. They started something that day in Acts 2 that's been going for 2,000 years. Now there are billions who follow Who they followed. Now there are churches and hospitals and orphanages and schools and soup kitchens and food banks and clothing banks and pregnancy centers and adoption agencies. Now there are water wells and homeless shelters and addiction centers. Now there are people who love and care and help and reach out. Now there is hope and faith and a future. Now it's all different.

I'm so glad they didn't care. I'm so glad they didn't cower before the words and the wounds and the ridicule that came from others. I'm so glad they didn't quit just because someone else didn't get it or didn't like it or made fun of them. After all, in the end, it doesn't matter what they say. It just doesn't matter.

I wish I had some more. A lot more. If I did, I could really help people. I could make a difference in their lives. If I just had some more. You know, money. But since I don't, I can't help people. After all, that's the only thing people need.

They don't need encouragement. Or love. Or care or concern or wise counsel. They don't need a friend or a smile or a compliment. They don't need a recommendation for a job or a pat on the back or a listening ear. Or do they?

I'm so glad those two guys didn't walk away from that crippled man because they didn't have any money. The crippled man was begging for money and the two guys didn't have any. But they had something he really needed. So they gave it to him. They gave him Jesus. The one named Peter said, "Silver or gold I do not have, but what I have I give you. In the name of Jesus of Nazareth, walk." And he did.

The truth is that money can be used for good and noble purposes. It can be used to help people in real and tangible ways. So if you have money, give it. Bless people with it. Change their circumstances. Give them a hand-up.

But if you don't have money, you can still give. Boy, can you give! Give them hope and joy and peace. Give them a friend and a future and a focus. Give them meaning. And purpose. And a life that matters. Today, in the middle of their sorrow and their struggles and their hopelessness, give them what you have. Give them Jesus.

Confession time. I don't always want to do the right thing. Even when I clearly know what the right thing is. Sometimes I want to do the wrong thing. Or the destructive thing. Or the disobedient thing.

Sometimes I want to do the wrong thing because the right thing doesn't make sense. Like that guy Joseph. He fell in love, bought a ring, and popped the question. She said yes and they began making plans for the wedding. It would be simple. A nice ceremony at their church with the reception in the fellowship hall. Things were good.

Then one day he received surprising news. Shocking news, actually. His fiancé was pregnant. That was pretty bad, but what made it a million times worse was the fact that he had never slept with her. Ever.

He was angry. And embarrassed. How could she do that to him? They hadn't even made it to the altar and she had already cheated on him. There was no way he would marry such a woman.

And then he had the dream. A very strange dream. An angel appeared to him and told him to marry his fiancé because she had not cheated on him but was pregnant as a result of the miraculous power of God. Yeah, right.

But not only that, the child his fiancé was carrying was a special child who would do amazing things. He would save people. From their sins.

So what did he do? According to this guy named Matthew, "He did what the angel of the Lord had commanded him and took Mary home as his wife."

He did it. He did what God wanted him to do. He was obedient under bizarre circumstances that made no sense.

Seems like God is still doing that. You know, asking us to do things that make no sense. To forgive people who have hurt us. To love people who have harmed us. To go the extra mile. To consider others better than ourselves. To die to self.

It's hard to do these things sometimes. But there are those who do. And I admire them so. There are those who do the right thing simply because it's the right thing to do. Even when every fiber of their being is crying out to do the opposite. Even when the flesh longs for disobedience, for revenge, for self, for destruction. And the flesh is very strong. And very powerful.

But there are people who take the high road rather than the low road. You know them and I know them. They choose to live rather than die. They choose to love rather than hate. They choose to continue rather than quit. They choose His way rather than the enemy's way.

And our world is a little better because of them.

I hate rules. Always have. They're often arbitrary and reactive and restrictive. They're bureaucratic and confining. They restrain creativity and make for a boring life. I just don't like them.

But we have a rule in our family. Had it for years. The rule goes like this: no one in our family will receive gifts at Christmas that are of greater monetary value than what we give to Jesus. That's it. That's the rule.

It's never made sense to me that we would celebrate someone's birthday by giving a lot of gifts to ourselves. Who does that? Can you imagine going to someone's birthday party and announcing, "Happy Birthday! Wait 'til you see what I got myself for your birthday. It's big! And expensive! And all for me!"

Sounds crazy, but it's what many of us do at Christmas every year. We celebrate the birth of Jesus by giving ourselves presents. That we don't need. And can't afford. We are strange people.

But maybe this year could be different. Maybe you could start a rule. A gift-giving rule. Maybe this year you could give a gift, not to yourself, but to Jesus, the One whose birth we are supposedly celebrating. What kind of gift? The possibilities are endless. Give through your church or a charitable organization. Help someone in your community who is struggling.

My family is giving money to help build a house for a Haitian pastor who lives in a tiny, two-room house with his 11 family members. That family's life is going to be changed dramatically. Not only that, but with his basic needs met, the pastor will be in a far better position to continue helping us help the 6,000 people in his village who have no electricity, no running water, and not much of anything else. That pastor is going to help us as we build a new Hope Center in his village that will provide medical care, dental care, new housing, jobs, education for the children, clean water, agriculture enhancements, and so much more.

It just seems that a gift to that Haitian pastor, given to celebrate the birth of Jesus, will be a lot more pleasing to the Father than more stuff for ourselves. So this year, give yourself something new. Give yourself a rule. A rule that will not only change someone else's life, but just might change yours too.

They left last week. Again. And now it's late Friday afternoon. I did all the work I plan to do for the day. And so I went upstairs to straighten their empty rooms.

There's clutter everywhere. I picked up the trash, straightened the bedspreads, saw the results of their summer back home. And then I got nostalgic. Sad even. Because they're gone. Our twin boys went back to college—separate colleges—for another year.

I don't begrudge them. It's supposed to be this way. They should go and grow and make new friends and dream new dreams. They should take all that we gave them and find out who they are and who they're going to be. If they didn't go and do and become, I would feel like a failure. I would tell them to go. So it's right they left again.

But I can still be sad. On occasion. Not for long and not in a depressed kind of way. But in an I-can't-believe-it's-over kind of way. And they are over. Those growing up years have passed. They were good and fun. We watched them grow. We taught them the best we could. We loved them and invested in them. Spent endless time and energy and money. On them.

And now we continue to watch. Just from farther away. Oh, we talk and text. They still need us, just not as much.

We love that they love their schools and their new lives. We'll go see them this fall. On the weekends at ball games for one. For plays and musicals for the other. We'll take them out to eat. Which they seem to like. And we'll catch up and try not to be too nosey. But we want to know. We want to know everything. What they're doing and what they're learning and who they're meeting and how they are. We just want to know. Because we remember. We remember when they learned to walk and when they played baseball and when we were all on vacation together. We remember the night of the big game and the days of long track meets. We remember the friends and the laughter and the first cars. We remember it all. And that's why we want to know.

And that's what I'm thinking on this Friday afternoon.

I can't relate. I don't get it. Never experienced it and don't understand it. But a lot of people do. They get it, they have experienced it, and many live it out daily. Many, many, many.

What is it? This quote I read today: "The most damaging statements that have ever been said about us are those things we have said about ourselves to ourselves. Many people have a never-ending loop of self-talk that berates them for being foolish, stupid, a failure, a loser."

I am aware this quote is a daily reality for countless people. But I don't understand. I would never tell myself that I am foolish or stupid or a failure or a loser. Never. Why would I do that? Makes no sense to me. Others may say that about me, but I would never join them in such harmful negativity.

Why is this self-abuse a strange concept to me? This is the point of today's devotional: my parents. They always told me I was smart and capable and talented and full of endless potential. Not in an everybody-gets-a-trophy kind of way. When I struck out in Little League, they didn't tell me I had done great and would be a Major League star one day. But they spent the years of my childhood affirming me, encouraging me, expecting good and right things from me, rewarding achievement, and giving comfort during times of difficulty. They never once called me foolish or stupid or a failure or a loser.

Please don't misunderstand. I was punished when I needed to be punished, corrected when I needed to be corrected, and not allowed to become a spoiled brat who thought he was more important than everyone else. But my parents instilled in me a healthy sense of self-worth. That I was a child of the King. That I would be loved by them no matter what. That I could achieve what I set my mind to achieve if I was willing to study, be disciplined, and work hard. And since they were my parents, I believed them. And I still do.

Parents, you have incredible power over your children. Your words matter. Some of those words will never be forgotten. So always correct your children when they are going astray, but never attack their character or their bodies or their minds or who they are as a person. Instead, build them up, encourage them, and believe in them.

No, I don't get it. And I thank God and my parents that I don't.

It was so simple, yet so profound. He wrote it in a letter in the spring of 1945 somewhere on German soil. Maybe in a foxhole.

Who was he? He was a soldier. A patriot. A man of honor and courage. A Christian. He was a young man with a wife and six-year-old daughter back home in the States. He had been gone for three years, so his little girl could not remember him. She never would.

On April 5, 1945, he was killed in battle fighting against evil and tyranny, fighting for freedom and hope and a future. He fought for his wife and daughter, his mother and father, his friends and his country. Who was he? His name was Horace. Horace Yelverton. And he was my grandfather.

His daughter, my mother, would never see him again. But he left her with something. He left her with his own words, words he had written to her and to her mother. Words that mattered then and continue to matter today. 73 years ago, he wrote the following words in one of his letters home: "I made up my mind long ago to live right."

That was it. That was the statement. Those were the words that were so simple yet filled with so much meaning.

At some point in the past, he made a decision. He determined he would live in a way that honored God. He would live with honesty and integrity. He would live with honor and humility. He would work hard and treat others fairly. He would live right.

Of course, he had no way of knowing the impact of his decision to live right. He didn't know his little girl would grow up and go to college and become a teacher. He didn't know she would spend 32 years teaching the poor and the downtrodden. He didn't know she would marry a pastor, serve in churches for over 50 years, teach Sunday School to hundreds and hundreds, write a column read by thousands for over twenty years, and give birth to two boys. He didn't know his two grandsons would marry and have five children between them. He didn't know his little girl and his son-in-law and his grandsons and their wives and their children would one day make up their minds to live right. He didn't know. But on that day in April of 1945 when he drew his last breath he did not die in vain. He left for his family, a family he would never know, the gift of freedom, and a legacy of living right.

So on this Memorial Day, I honor Horace Yelverton and his sacrifice—his awful, noble, and beautiful sacrifice. And I thank God for a grandfather who made up his mind long ago to live right.

It matters. It really, really, really matters. As much as anything in this life, it matters. I saw it first-hand recently. We had all gathered at my house for my daughter's high school graduation. My dad. My mom. My brother and his wife. Their two children. Me. My wife and our three children, including the graduate. After the ceremony, we went to my house, had a huge meal, and sat and talked and celebrated my daughter. And that's when it hit me. Family matters. A good and strong and godly family really matters. And men—godly men, strong men—matter a great deal.

I looked at my children and my niece and nephew and I realized they were not alone. They don't exist in a vacuum. They were surrounded by men. Strong men. A grandfather and a father and an uncle. Men with convictions and passion. Men with a strong work ethic. Men who have worked hard, played hard, pursued life. Men who have made mistakes but kept going, kept striving, stayed in the game. Men who have accomplished much. Men who are people of faith, the Christian faith. Men who stick by their wives and children. Men who provide for their families. Men who aren't going anywhere. Men.

And I realized my children and my brother's children are recipients of a heritage, a past, a history. They are not alone. They are not alone. They. Are. Not. Alone. In a tough, challenging, difficult world, they are not alone. Our children have support and encouragement and discipline and accountability. They can stand tall with pride and confidence knowing they are part of a family that is far from perfect but is together. That when the world turns its back on them, their family will still be there. No matter what.

I saw it that day. Family matters. Men matter. They really do.

I have three children. They're all in college. Three different colleges. They seem to be adjusting well to their respective schools. Actually, they love their schools. And I'm glad.

It doesn't happen often, but it did two days ago. I was alone for a few moments and I thought of my children and the years we had when they were growing up. I thought of their laughter and their energy. I thought of the trips we went on and all those nights at the dinner table. And I thought of how quickly it went by. And I thought of how much I love them.

For a split second I wanted to go back. I wanted to do it again. I wanted to hear them cheer when I come home from work. I wanted to hear the excitement in their voices and see the sparkle in their eyes when they discover something new. I wanted to do it again.

You see, it was different then. He used to hold my hand when we walked across the yard. His brother used to organize plays in our house. She used to crawl in my lap.

And now things are different. He doesn't hold my hand anymore. His brother doesn't organize plays in our house. She doesn't crawl in my lap.

And today I miss that.

I love it. I really do. Sometimes it's strange and difficult and frustrating. But I love it. In fact, I wouldn't have it any other way. What is it? Marriage, of course.

Marriage is great. God was so smart when He came up with this idea of a man and a woman being united together for a lifetime. What's so great about marriage? Lots of things.

In marriage, you have someone to live with. Someone to come home to. Someone to eat with and talk with and do life with. Someone to make a home with.

In marriage, you create children and raise a family. You go to ball games and concerts and plays. You go on vacations and watch them grow up and change and mature. You watch them succeed and fail and try. You cheer for them and hope for them and cry for them. You worry about them. Often. And along the way you have that other person who helped you create those children and who loves them as much as you do.

In marriage, you have someone who's on your side, in your corner, pulling for you. Someone who has your back no matter what. Someone who's going to be there when you fall down and when you mess up and when you make a mistake.

In marriage, you have that physical intimacy that you share with no one else. That intimacy that is good and right and comforting and, well, just marvelous.

In marriage, you have someone to help carry the burdens when life is bad. Someone to lean on and count on. Someone to be there for better or worse, in sickness and in health.

In marriage, you have someone to call, someone to expect, someone to miss when they're away. You have someone to sit by and someone's hand to hold.

In marriage, you have someone to look after, someone for whom you are responsible, someone to bless. Someone to love.

In marriage, you have someone to grow old with. Someone who knows you better than anyone. Someone who, over the years, you come to cherish above all others.

Marriage? I love it. I really do.

I can't figure it out. I've tried. For years I've tried. For almost 30 years I've tried and tried and tried. Sometimes I've tried harder than other times. But I can't figure it out. Marriage. Marriage is the most incredible, difficult, wonderful, challenging, comforting, frustrating, marvelous, baffling relationship in the world. The good times can be really good. The bad times can be really bad.

I love being married. I can't imagine not being married. My marriage, apart from my faith, is the most important part of my life. By far. But just when you think you've gotten a handle on marriage something goes awry. There's a disagreement, a misunderstanding, or a full-blown fight. It's like golf. You have the best round of your life and you think you've finally figured it out then the next round you shoot your highest score in years.

Why is marriage so difficult, even when you have a great spouse like I have? It's because of all the challenges. Like money. And sex. Like the basic differences between men and women. There are different expectations coming into the marriage. There's baggage from previous relationships. There are differences in the way you were reared.

So what do you do? Here are some suggestions. These are for couples in which both partners want to have a good, healthy marriage. If one party is not interested or if there are drugs, abuse, or adultery, then those are much larger issues that must be addressed separately and in far greater detail. I read the suggestions below in a blog called One Flesh Marriage. The parts in bold are from the authors of the blog.

1. **Focus on who your spouse is instead of focusing on who your spouse is not.** I can spend all my time thinking about my wife's faults and what she does wrong and how she could improve, or I could spend my time thinking about the many good things she does and what a blessing she is in my life and how God has designed her. I can focus on her many great attributes. It's a choice.

2. **Be intentional about blessing your spouse every week.** It won't happen automatically. Think about it. Make some plans. It doesn't have to be expensive. What can you do this week to bless your spouse?

3. **Plan a getaway and let nothing stop you.** Go somewhere. Get away from the routine. Focus on one another.

4. **Make sex a priority and engage regularly.** Sex is the one thing that I do only with my wife. Most all other activities I do with my wife as well as others. Sex is different. And special. It's when I'm most vulnerable. For most men, it is absolutely, unequivocally, without question, essential to a good marriage. It's not merely a nice addition to the marriage whenever you get around to it. It's vital. To quote a passage from the book, "for women only":

"In a very deep way, your man often feels isolated and burdened by secret feelings of inadequacy. Making love with you assures him that you find him desirable, salves a deep sense of loneliness, and gives him the strength to face the world with confidence. And, of course, sex also makes him feel loved—in fact, he can't feel completely loved without it."

Wives, you wield incredible power over the well-being of your husband, especially in this area. If I am having good, regular sex with my wife, then everything is OK in my world. It just is. I am content and confident and happy. If that part of my marriage is not good, then I am angry, frustrated, and resentful. Everything else in my life can be going well, but it won't matter.

5. **Do something specific to grow your marriage.** One example is attending a marriage retreat together.

6. **Keep growing in your Christian faith.** If I am maturing in my faith, then the fruit of the Spirit (Galatians 5:22-23) will be evident in my life. Things like love, joy, peace, patience, kindness, goodness, faithfulness, gentleness, and self-control. Clearly, these attributes will make me a better spouse.

7. **Laugh together.** Have fun. Enjoy life. No one wants to be around a sourpuss.

Stan Buckley

One other thing. Don't quit. Work at your marriage. Get help. See a trained marriage counselor. It's worth it. Make the effort. Be selfless. Enjoy your spouse.

I love being married. Wouldn't trade it for anything. And I'm still trying to figure it out.

It wasn't what she expected. Or signed up for. But it's what happened. Twenty-nine year ago, she married a young man who had just finished his first year of law school. She would work the next two years in a job she didn't really like. But she did it. Every day. So they could eat. She knew it would be worth it. He made good grades. Was selected for the law review. He would get a good job with a nice salary. They would buy a house and have kids and go to church and have a good life.

And that's what happened. For a while. He got a good job with a good firm. They moved to a new town and a new neighborhood and a nice first home. They found a great church and settled in and everything was good. Then she became pregnant. With twins. It was very exciting and she came home from work.

But then he became restless. He told her one day he felt a calling on his life. From God. He thought he should go back for more school and become a pastor. It wasn't what she expected. It wasn't part of the plan. There had been no mention of this when they dated or when they were engaged. And he told her he had to do it. He had to do it or his soul would shrivel and die. But he couldn't do it without her. So she said OK.

And he went to school. Two hours away In New Orleans. Day after day for three years. Back and forth. After the first year, he received a call from a church in a rural setting where she knew no one. And he moved them there. All four of them. It wasn't what she expected.

But it was good. Really good. She grew to love that place and that church and those people. Especially those people. And she became pregnant. Again. This time it was a girl. A beautiful, sweet, wonderful girl.

But it came to an end, as it always does. And they moved. They moved to a town. With a courthouse and a community college and a nice home. It was, it seemed to them, a Mayberry kind of place where everyone knew everyone. And they liked it. A lot. And it wasn't what she expected.

Then another church called. And it was different. Much different. It was very big and it was in a city and it was downtown. And her family of five lived in the suburbs and drove to church. Her children grew older and taller and more active. And it wasn't what she expected.

Then one day the heart of the man she married was grabbed by something else. A place. A country. A people. He went to Haiti and he knew he had to do something about all the poverty and all the despair and all the hopelessness. He had to. He couldn't see it and know it and do nothing about it. He just couldn't. So he got this crazy idea that he said came from God that they would build a community on that island. A community with food and clean water and housing and jobs and medical care and a church. And she didn't laugh at him. She didn't tell him he was crazy or had misunderstood or had gone too far. She didn't tell him it wouldn't work or it would cost too much or it would never happen.

She just believed in him. She thought, with God's help, he could do it. She thought, with the help of his friends and his church, a difference could be made. And so he set out to do it. To build it. And then he told her one day that he would leave the big church and try to help the people on the island full-time. He would devote his time and energy and efforts to helping them help themselves. And it wasn't what she expected.

And for 29 years, through all the changes and all the schools and all the jobs and all the children and all the everything, she stood by his side. And she never left. And she never told him he couldn't do it. Not once.

And he was blessed. For 29 years he was blessed. Very blessed indeed.

She wasn't angry. At least not at me. She could have been. Perhaps, she should've been. After all, she had spent Sunday night packing after a long, challenging, and traveling weekend. She had gotten up at 3:00 in the morning on Monday to get ready and we left our house at 4:00.

We were excited. It had been over a year since she had been with me to Haiti and we were finally going. So much had happened since her last visit. So much improvement, so much ministry, so many lives blessed.

Jewell, my wife, was headed to Haiti. We were going to spend two days at a retreat for our Haitian and American staff and their spouses. We were going into the mountains to Thoman to see the progress on the new Hope Center. We would spend the final night in Galette Chambon at our original Hope Center. I was so excited to have her by my side. It was going to be great.

We arrived at the airport at 4:30 a.m., checked our bags at the airline counter, then headed for the security line. As we approached the TSA agent, Jewell took out her passport. That's when it happened. That's when it all fell apart. She looked at me in disbelief, held up her passport and said, "It's expired."

In an instant, I knew. I knew there was nothing we could do. We couldn't fix it in the next 30 seconds before we stepped in front of the TSA agent. There was nothing we could do. So I said, "You can't go." And as I said those words, my heart sank. I wanted her to go. I wanted her to see all that had been done since her last visit. I wanted her by my side.

The couple we were with took out the keys to their vehicle that was parked in long-term parking. She would drive that vehicle home. Alone.

It was my fault. You see, I'm the keeper of the passports in our family. For years, whenever we have traveled, immediately after showing our passports, I have taken them all up for safekeeping. I keep them at home in a special place. I'm the keeper of the passports. So I should have known. I should have been paying attention. It was my fault.

And that's when grace entered the picture. She had every right to be angry with me. But she never showed anger. She never said the obvious: that it was my fault and I'm the keeper of the passports and if I'm going to be in charge then I need to be in charge and take care of things. I think she knew. She knew I didn't do it on purpose. She knew the retreat was very important and I needed to focus on it. She knew the other couple traveling with us needed to have a good experience.

So she didn't lash out and she didn't pout. She just went home, caught up on her sleep, went to work the next few days, and picked us up at the airport at the end of the week.

Marriage is a wonderful, difficult, blissful, challenging, complicated sort of thing. But three weeks ago she didn't get angry. And I am blessed.

Do you believe it? Do you? Do you really believe it?

We were walking through the halls of the ICU on the way to my dad's room. It was 2:45 a.m. A few minutes earlier, we had received the call we knew was coming. He was dead.

So we made our way to his room. There were five of us—my mother, my brother, his wife, my wife, and me. As we walked, I said to them, "Either we believe what we say we believe or we don't."

We've always said we believe. We've spent decades going to church, worshiping God, reading the Scriptures, studying the Bible. Countless hours have been devoted to our Christian faith. We've always said we believe.

We've sung hymns about heaven, we've celebrated the Resurrection, we've talked about seeing others who have gone before us. We've always said we believe.

But do we really? When the chips are down, when reality hits, when our hearts are broken and we don't understand, do we really believe?

After all, it's easy to believe when things are good. It's easy to believe when everyone is healthy. It's easy to believe when problems are few. But what about when things are not good? What about those times of heartache? Do we believe then? Do we believe when we're walking down that hallway to see the body of our husband, our dad, our father-in-law? Do we believe when we know he won't talk and he won't get up and he won't go home with us? Do we believe then?

As it turns out, we do. We believe Jesus when He said, "Because I live, you too shall live."

We believe Him when He said, "I am the Resurrection and the life. He who believes in me will live, even though he dies."

We believe Jesus when He told His disciples that He was going to prepare a place for them and that He would come back and receive them so they could be with Him.

We believe that Jesus was raised from the dead on the third day, forever defeating Satan, and death, and hell.

We believe the answer to Job's question, "If a man dies will he live again," is a resounding yes!

We believe the Apostle Paul when he wrote that to be absent from the body is to be present with the Lord.

We believe Paul's words that to depart this earth and go and be with the Lord is better by far.

We believe we will see our loved ones again and they will know us and we will know them.

We believe the greatest longing of every redeemed soul is to see the face of God and that one day we will.

I made a mistake at the beginning of this little devotional. I said my dad was dead. He's really not. The great evangelist of another day, Dwight L. Moody, once told a large audience, "One day you will pick up a newspaper and read that Dwight L. Moody is dead. Don't you believe it, for on that day I will be more alive than I've ever been."

We miss my dad. He was an amazing man who lived life to the fullest. We are saddened that he is not with us right now. But in the midst of our sorrow, we believe. We believe what we say we believe. We just do. And it has made all the difference.

It was strange. I had never done it before. I bought a one-way ticket.

Why would I buy a one-way ticket? Because he's moving. He's not merely visiting. He's moving. One of our sons is moving to New York City.

His mother is sad. After all, you can't jump in a car and get to New York in an hour or two. She's worried about holidays and family gatherings and when we will see him again. She's worried about his finances and his friends and his faith. She wants him to get a paying job while he looks for his real job. She's worried about her son.

I have concerns, but I'm really kind of excited for him. I see his move as a big adventure. I see the possibilities and the challenges and the fun. I see a whole new world. I see the chance for him to pursue a dream for which he has spent the last four years preparing. Plus, he's been there many times. And he has quite a few friends there, some from our hometown and many from his college.

I suppose this is just another change in life. They seem to keep coming, these changes. And there doesn't seem to be much you can do about it. One day you're in high school, the next day it's your 30th reunion. One day you start that first job, the next day you're thinking about retirement. One day you're bringing them home from the hospital, the next day they're moving to New York. How did that happen? And how did it happen so fast?

I'm not sure what to do about all these changes. Based on past experience, it seems there will be more changes. Do I try to hang on to the past? Do I fight the future? Do I learn some lessons and accept the new realities?

I'm not sure. I just know it was strange and I had never done it before. I bought a one-way ticket.

Do you have a daughter? I have a daughter. She is in college and this morning I was thinking of her. I was thinking of her future. And I was thinking of how one decision will impact her life more than most of the other decisions she will make. I was thinking about the person she may marry one day. Because of the importance of this decision, I shared some thoughts with her. This is what I said:

I want to remind you how important it is to marry the right person. You know the rule: don't marry a moron. That's true, but there's so much more to it than that.

The person you marry will impact your life every single day. That's right, every single day.

Make sure you marry a Christian, a man who loves God and wants to serve Him and grow in his faith. That's number one.

Make sure you marry a man of honesty and integrity. You don't want to spend your life wondering every day if your spouse is lying to you or cheating on you or being dishonest in any way.

Make sure you marry a man with a strong work ethic. There's nothing worse than a lazy man who is not willing to do whatever it takes to provide for his family.

Make sure you marry a man who has no problems with alcohol or drugs. Living with those issues would be a never-ending nightmare for you and your children.

Also, do not be impressed by some young man simply because he is handsome or popular or comes from a wealthy family. Be very careful if he comes from a wealthy family. We know many outstanding young people who come from wealthy families. However, many times a young person from a wealthy family lives a disastrous life. If you find yourself interested in a young man from a wealthy family, make sure he does not feel entitled or that he doesn't feel superior to others. Make sure he has not been given everything his entire life and is therefore lazy and soft and unwilling to work. A young man who has never earned anything but has had everything handed to him is someone you should avoid at all costs.

You're not looking for someone who is perfect, but there should be some things that are essential. There are some things on which you should not compromise: faith, integrity, strong work ethic, and no issues with alcohol or drugs. These are essential.

So, know who you are and the kind of life you want for yourself and your future children. Don't marry someone thinking you will change him. That's a huge mistake. Most people's personalities and habits are well-formed by the time they reach 21.

Finally, as we've discussed before, don't give yourself physically to some foolish guy with whom you will soon part company. Save that for your future husband and give the gift of yourself to him on your wedding day.

I love you. You are beautiful, smart, and will make a great wife and mother one day.

She died Sunday. Got a text from a friend. Made me sad. Memories, wonderful memories, flooded my mind. We loved her. I loved her. She was Ms. Wilma and she played an important role in the life of my family. For that, I shall be forever grateful.

I'll be speaking at her funeral this week. Hope to honor her and tell what she did for my family and me. Because it mattered.

What did she do? She did two things. First, she loved my children. She adored them. Thought they were great. Looked after them. Took care of them. Spoiled them. Rotten. If someone loves your children, you love them back. Forever.

Second, she blessed my wife and me in an amazing way. We were serving there at our first church. In the country. When we moved there, our twin boys were about two. Jewell would give birth to our daughter a year later.

Ms. Wilma said to us: "If you ever need to go somewhere or want to do something, call me to keep the kids. Anytime." And she meant it. Was adamant about it. Said she would be mad if we didn't call her. So we did. All the time. We would go eat Chinese on Sunday nights after church and Ms. Wilma kept the kids. We ate catfish most Thursday nights with two other couples. Ms. Wilma kept the kids. We could go and do and take care of things because Ms. Wilma kept the kids.

Sometimes, she would keep them at our house. She would bring a bag for them. Every time. Filled with candy and chocolate. And she would give them a soft drink. You think they loved Ms. Wilma?

Usually she kept them at her house. They would play outside and play inside. She would fix them snacks and then lunch and then more snacks. They would play games and have fun and just be children. Her husband would be there and sometimes her grown grandchildren and the would play with the children too. And we would rest. Or have a little time alone. Or enjoy the company of adults.

We moved away from that first church and that community we loved so much. But Ms. Wilma never forgot the children. Every year on their birthday she would send them a two dollar bill for every year they had been alive.

God was kind to us when He brought Ms. Wilma into our lives. In a busy and hectic time, she gave us rest and peace. She wasn't famous. Or wealthy. Or scholarly. She just loved us. And it was the greatest gift.

You want to. I know you do, because we all do. We want to leave something of value to our children and our grandchildren. We want to bless them. And there are lots of ways to do so. We can leave them property or money. We can teach them a trade or a skill. But perhaps there is an even better way.

There was this guy named Solomon who was supposed to be the wisest person who ever lived. He said this: "The righteous man leads a blameless life; blessed are his children after him."

He was right, this wise man. The best way to bless your children is to live a blameless life, a godly life. Not a perfect life. Not a sinless life. But a life of honor and integrity.

I knew my great-grandfather. We called him Gran. He was a man of integrity. He wasn't wealthy or famous. He simply lived a good life, took care of his family, was involved in his church, loved his country, and did what was right. His son, my grandfather, did the same. Worked hard, loved God, loved his country, obeyed the law, did what was right. My own father did the same. Worked hard, loved God, loved family, loved his country, and did what is right. Now, none of these three men have been perfect. None of them. But when you look at their lives as a whole, they have lived blameless and godly lives. As a result, I am blessed. Greatly blessed.

I am blessed because I don't have to be ashamed of my family. I am blessed because I know how to live a good and proper life. I am blessed because I can be proud of those who have gone before me. I am blessed because I was taught to know and love God. I am blessed because I was taught right from wrong. I am blessed because I was never taught to lie or cheat or steal. I am blessed because I can pass these same values on to my children and grandchildren. I am blessed.

So, if you can leave a monetary blessing for your children, that's great. Do it wisely. But of far greater importance will be the godly blessing of a righteous life. Give them that. And they will be blessed. Greatly blessed.

I have no one to call. I know I'm supposed to call. I always have. But not anymore. I have no one to call.

This Sunday is Father's Day. It's a day to celebrate fatherhood. It's a day to call your dad and check in and let him know you're thinking about him. But as of March 27, 2017, I have no one to call on Father's Day.

March 27 was the day he died. It was the day a man with an outsized personality and a zest for life left this earth. He breathed his last and now he's not here.

Because he's not here, there is much that is missing. His laughter is gone. His planning-of-trips is gone. His enthusiasm for life is gone. His recollection of people and events is gone.

His commentary on sports is gone. His preaching is gone. His support is gone. His encouragement is gone. His stubbornness is gone. His can-do attitude is gone. His optimism is gone.

But maybe it's not. Maybe it's not all gone. The more I think of it, most of it's still here. It's just here in me. And my brother. And my children and my brother's children. And hopefully it will be in their children as they live their lives to the fullest and pass on those traits they saw in their grandfather.

As they rear their children, hopefully they'll remember a grandfather who was not content to sit passively while life happened around him, but instead embraced life and its challenges and opportunities. Hopefully, they'll be stubborn enough to do the right thing and hold firm and not bow to the passing fads of culture. Hopefully, they'll have fun and work hard and stand for the truth. Hopefully, they'll love God and His church and serve Him faithfully for a lifetime.

No, it's not gone. His good traits are alive and well. But still, this Sunday I have no one to call.

Would I do it? Would I make the effort, go through all the trouble, spend all my time and energy and resources? Would I be so excited about it? You know, if no one noticed. If no one knew. If I could get no credit and no recognition. Would I still do it?

There was this guy with a funny first name. Oswald. Who names their child Oswald? Well, Mr. and Mrs. Chambers did. And little Oswald turned out to be quite the thinker. Quite the writer. In fact, he wrote a book called *My Utmost for His Highest*. And it's been treasured by lots of people. Lots and lots and lots of people.

So, back to the question. Would I serve and sacrifice and go if no one knew? If I wasn't going to be congratulated and affirmed? If my efforts were not made public? Oswald wrote, "The real test of a saint is not one's willingness to preach the gospel, but one's willingness to do something like washing the disciples' feet—that is, being willing to do those things that seem unimportant in human estimation but count as everything to God."

Is it enough to be quietly obedient? Is it enough to see needs met even if there's no fanfare and no recognition? Is it enough to see lives changed even if no one else notices? Oswald said, "A New Testament saint is not one who merely proclaims the gospel, but one who becomes broken bread and poured-out wine in the hands of Jesus Christ for the sake of others."

Would I do it? If no one knew?

She heard about it. She had the means. She did something.

I met him two weeks ago in an impoverished mountain community in Haiti. He is paralyzed from the waist down. Sits in a wheelchair all day long. He looked to be in his 50s, but it's hard to tell. Something happened, something terrible. There was a pop and he lost the use of his legs. He's been to nine hospitals but nothing has changed.

I saw his wife hoeing in a garden. It looked to be a rock garden because the plot of land is covered in rocks. But she was trying. Really trying.

She took me to their house and that's where I saw him. They have four children. Three are school age. The fourth, a daughter, died recently and left them with four grandchildren to care for. They now have seven children to look after. And no job (because there aren't any), no income (no disability check will come each month), and no hope (how will they survive).

I looked at them and didn't know what to do. I couldn't solve their problems. I couldn't make him walk. So I asked if I could pray for them. They're Christians and they said yes. So I prayed. I asked God for strength and healing and blessings. I said amen and lifted my eyes. Tears were rolling down his cheeks. He seemed to be a proud man, in a good way, and now he can't work his garden to provide food for his family.

She texted me last week. She had heard about this family. Wanted to know what they needed. I told her it would be great if two or three of the kids could be sponsored to go to the school there in the village. I told her it's $37 per month, $444 per year, for each child. They would get to eat every day and learn to read and write and do math. They would get a uniform and be like the other kids and have fun. And those would be two less meals for that mother to somehow provide each day.

She responded. I couldn't believe it. She asked if all seven needed to be sponsored. I said no. One is already in school but six are not. She said to sign them all up. All six of them. She would send a check the next day. And she did.

They're in school now. All those children. I got word the mother was very excited when she got the news. She was thrilled to hear all these children would be in school each day. And they would eat. And get a uniform. And learn. And have a chance.

She heard about it. She had the means. She did something.

Been thinking about this Easter weekend while also thinking about our work in Haiti. When I think about the crucifixion, I think of words like Painful. Unfair. Death. Hope lost.

When I think about Haiti immediately after the earthquake, the same words come to mind. Painful. Unfair. Death. Hope lost.

And then came Sunday. The stone was rolled away. He was alive. And there was great joy. The women, the disciples, they were amazed. It was a miracle! The greatest one of all. He was alive. Jesus . . . changed . . . everything.

Then my mind returns to our work in Haiti. I think about The Hope Center. And the clean water wells. And the medical care and the dental care. I think about the houses and the gardens and the jobs. I think about the church and the orphanage. I think about Bible schools and Bible studies. I think about Nurse Tony and Wife Mickie and Haitian Pastor Daniel and hundreds of Christians who have gone and loved and shared and cared. Why? Because He is alive. He lives in you and me and all who have gone. And there has been great joy. The moms and the dads. The little children. The tent dwellers and the sick. The ones with hurting mouths and hungry stomachs. There has been great joy. As one of our Haitian partners once said, "It's a miracle!"

It's true: He is alive. Hope is not lost. Jesus has changed everything . . . again.

I didn't want to tell him. But I thought I should. It was kind of embarrassing, sort of a confession. So we sat down and I told him. I said, "Pastor Mathurin, I live in a big house. A really big house." He said, "I thought you did." I kept going. "Most of the people I know live in big houses. My family, my friends, the people I go to church with. Everyone you will see in a few days lives in a big house."

I had to tell him because this Friday Pastor Mathurin will be coming to America with me from Haiti. It will be his first flight. First time off his island. And it's going to be different.

Pastor Mathurin lives in a remote village in the mountains. Far away from civilization. No electricity. No running water. Just houses made of mud or block. A dirt road. His family of nine lives in a house the size of my keeping room.

I can't wait for him to land on American soil. I can't wait for him to see all that America is and all that America has to offer. The roads and the lights and the stores. The opportunities. The fact that you can get anything you want at any time. Wait 'til he sees our grocery store and the endless food at cheap prices. Wait 'til he walks in our Super Store and sees more items than he can imagine. Wait 'til he sees the restaurants and the cars and the neighborhoods filled with big houses. Everywhere.

And the churches. Oh, wait 'til he sees the churches. Fine churches that hold hundreds, even thousands of people. Parking lots and kitchens and nurseries and fellowship halls. TV cameras in some, theater seats in others. Orchestras and praise bands. It will be different all right. Different from his one room church with wooden benches that have no backs. It will be different.

I'm not sure what to think about all this. This disparity between America and Haiti, between the rich and the poor, between my church and his church. I'm not sure what to think or do or conclude. You know, as a Christian.

Sometimes it doesn't seem fair. I'm no better than Mathurin. His children are just as precious as my children. His needs are like my needs. He loves the Lord as much as I do. Probably more.

Yet my world is very different from his. I'm never hungry. I never wonder whether my family will have food or shelter or transportation. I worry about my family, but not about the same things.

I wonder, as a Christian, do I have any duties, any responsibilities towards others? Towards the poor. Towards the hungry or the thirsty or the hurting or the suffering.

I'm not sure what to think. But on Friday, Pastor Mathurin is coming to America.

It was so funny. We laughed and we marveled and we had a great time. It was his first time. He had never done it before, much less seen anyone else do it. Bowling. That's right, bowling. There aren't many bowling alleys in his remote village in the mountains of Haiti. But last night, here in America, Pastor Mathurin went bowling.

He had a lot of questions. The first thing he wanted to know was who was putting up those pins. I gave him the answer I've given him a dozen times so far. Nobody. A machine does it. And when the ball just magically appeared again, the same ball that had just been rolled down the lane, he was amazed yet again.

He caught on quickly. An 8 in the first frame. One time he bowled, watched the ball roll slowly down the lane. When it struck most of the pins, he turned around with a huge grin and threw up both hands in victory. So funny. By the end of the night, he had scored a 77. Not bad for a first time.

It was a great night, but not because of the bowling. We could have been playing basketball or baseball, video games or checkers. Really, anything if those same people had been with us. You see, what made the night was the company we kept, the people who took us bowling. The ones who smiled and laughed and hugged and played.

They were nice. Very nice. They were kind and gentle. They thought little of themselves and much of others. They weren't haughty or rude or mean. And they love God. A lot. Not perfect, mind you. Just good folks.

They reminded me of so many others I have encountered doing this work in Haiti. Like Buddy, whose heart is as big as the moon. Like Margaret, who loves to help. Like Paul, who is kind and gentle and good. Like Paula, who has so much compassion. Like Craig, who is so easy to be around. Like Lee, who is always thinking of ways to help. Like Leyna, whose heart is filled with love. There's Jim, who involves others. And Bobby, who is a great encourager. There are just so many of them. I weep as I think about who they are and what they do and how they live.

They're from here. And there. This state. And that state. This church and the other church. They go and they give and they plan. They sacrifice and they care and they support. They pray. Often. Their lives are filled with the evidence of a God-centered life. Things like love and joy and peace. Patience, kindness, and goodness. Faithfulness and gentleness and self-control are part of who they are.

It is a joy to know these people. They have enriched my life. They make me better. And I am so thankful. These people—these God-loving, Jesus-following people—are making a difference. They're making a huge difference in the mountains of Haiti and . . . well, yes, in the bowling alleys of America.

Gustav's life was hopeless. His skin was charred. His house was destroyed. His daughter couldn't go to school.

There was a fire. And all was lost. Gustav had no resources to rebuild. He lived in a small block house in the mountains of Haiti and he had no steady job, no savings, nothing. So he found some discarded pieces of tin and made a small, square structure with a dirt floor. And that's where he and his family lived.

Even before the fire, his life was hard. Very hard. A village with no electricity and no running water and no jobs. And his daughter, who is 7 or 8, didn't go to school. Gustav couldn't afford it.

Then one day last summer, we arrived at the church near his burned-down home to hold a medical clinic. He heard we were coming, so he got there early. They came and got me and said I needed to see the man who had been burned. His arms looked like a piece of wood that had been in a fire for a long time. Black, crisp, partially peeled. Awful. Just awful.

But Kevin was there. God had sent Kevin on that day to that village to that church to see that man named Gustav. Kevin is a general surgeon from Meridian, Mississippi. Every Friday he does wound care. He had the exact training and the exact experience to treat Gustav. And he did.

I saw Gustav last week. His arms have healed. He looks so good. And last week God sent some more of His people to let Gustav know that He had not forgotten him. He had not abandoned him. And He never will.

This time God sent Jim. He sent Jim, who is from Birmingham, and Jim brought a bunch of his friends and they worked really, really hard and they worked alongside some other Haitians who received jobs that week and they built a house for Gustav and his family. And Gustav was very thankful and very happy. No longer does his family have to live on a dirt floor in a tin shack.

Recently something else happened to Gustav. He became a Christian. A Christ-follower. Saved by the power of the Living God. And every Saturday he can't wait to go to the New Believers class and learn more about this God who loves him.

Last Tuesday I was walking away from the construction site around 10:00 a.m. A little girl was walking beside me carrying a bucket. I asked my friend Terry who she was. Terry said she was the daughter of Gustav and she was going to the river to get water. Her name was Jusmithe. I asked why she wasn't in school. She needed to be learning to read and write and do math and science. She needed her mind expanded and her thoughts developed. She needed to grow intellectually and emotionally and spiritually. She needed an education. Terry said she wasn't in school because Gustav couldn't afford to send her to school and she had no sponsor.

In that moment I knew Jusmithe would never again miss school because she was poor. I knew there was no way she would grow up in intellectual darkness, doomed to a life of poverty and hopelessness. It couldn't happen. Not as long as God gave my wife and me breath and allowed us to live in the most prosperous country in the world. Not as long as we could sponsor her for $37 a month and that would pay for her tuition and her uniform and her books. And not as long as that would also provide her one meal every day. And not as long as her sponsorship would also feed 3 other children every day. Thirty-seven dollars a month. We spend more than that on one meal dining out with our children.

So I went to www.butgodministries.com and we sponsored Jusmithe. I went because I know the school and the teachers and the students. And because I'll be going back there countless times. And because my Sunday School class recently built 4 classrooms there. Because I know it's real and it works and it's been blessed by God.

Gustav's life was hopeless. His skin was charred. His house was destroyed. His daughter couldn't go to school.

But that Jesus who died on that cross and then walked out of that tomb sent His people and everything changed. And that's something to celebrate this Easter Sunday.

It's a road. A road. Just a road. We've all seem them. Driven on them. A road.

But really, it's so much more than a road. Just ask them. They'll gladly tell you. It's opportunity. It's economic development and a smoother ride and an easier way home. It's a safer place for people and especially vehicles. Car, trucks, motorcycles. Fewer blown tires and fewer blown shocks.

They asked for it. Over a year ago. "Could you help with the road?" I told them that was a tall order. I told them to pray that God would provide the knowledge and the equipment and the resources to fix the road. It would be harder, more complex than anything else we had done. And I didn't have a clue how to fix a two-mile road in the middle of nowhere on a poverty-stricken island.

But He knew. He knew when and how and with what. He wasn't confused or bewildered. After all, if you can put the stars in the sky and the water in the ocean, a little road in Haiti is no big deal.

So He is getting it done. With a dozer and a grader and skilled, volunteer, American, Christian workers, He's getting it done. Just like we have seen Him do countless times. He brought the engineer and the money and the workers. He brought it all together at the right time and now the road is being fixed.

You should have seen them. Hundreds of them. Standing and pointing and thrilled at the work being done. They are more excited about this road project than any other project we have attempted.

It's a miracle, really. Just another regular, ordinary, life-changing miracle. What fun!

Stan Buckley

We don't believe it. Oh, we know it intellectually. We've read about it. We've heard others talk about it. But we don't really believe it. At least not for us. It may be true for others. You know, for smarter people or wealthier people or more spiritual people. But not us.

I'm so glad he believed. Terry. Terry from Arkansas. He believed that one person could make a difference. I sat in our missionary house in Haiti two days ago and he told me about it. He wasn't boasting. Not Terry. Never heard him boast. Probably never will.

He's been working in the mountain village of Thoman in Haiti for a couple of years. Travels there several times a year to see how he can help. He said that a year ago he went into Port-au-Prince to meet with the folks at Compassion International. He was already sponsoring two Haitian children through them and he wanted to see if they would start sponsoring children in the remote area of Thoman. For a number of reasons it didn't work out.

As he was telling one Haitian lady what happened, she said, "You do it." So a year ago, he sat down with Pastor Mathurin on the steps of the house where Terry and I were talking. He told Mathurin that he would like to start a sponsorship program in Thoman. Mathurin asked him how many children would be sponsored. Terry told him three. A grand total of three. He said it was just his wife and him and they could only sponsor three. Mathurin wasn't fazed by the meager number. He said OK. We will sponsor three children in my village.

Terry then told me, "Stan, it's amazing what God can do. Today, one year later, over 200 children are being sponsored (over 860 in 2018). They get to attend school, have a uniform, receive school supplies, and have one good meal a day while at school."

There's a committee now. They interview the children and the families who are included in the sponsorship program. They administer the funds. And lives are being changed. I know. I was in Thoman last week. On two different days. And not only are children being sponsored, but Terry has now built 5 houses (over 65 in 2018) and a dorm (a Hope Center was built in 2015) for visiting teams. This week, Terry brought his pastor and some medical folks from his church and they are holding a medical clinic all week and completing the other two houses.

As I sat there talking with Terry on Friday, I thought about the fish. And the loaves. I was reminded that God can take little and make much. You see, Terry from Arkansas didn't have a big organization. He didn't have any organization. He didn't have wealthy supporters. He didn't have a network of people who could help.

But he had something more important. He had a willing heart. And a Great Big God. Terry was available. He was open. He knew what God was leading him to do and he did it. And somehow, some way, God multiplied his efforts and little children aren't nearly as hungry as they used to be.

It's funny that after all these years, we still don't believe. We're still afraid to say yes to His calling. We're still doubting that He could use us to start that ministry, to reach our community, to share His love in the inner-city, to see lives changed near and far. We still don't believe that He could use someone like us. But I have to tell you, after talking to Terry Friday afternoon . . . I believe.

I was sitting there. Overwhelmed. Getting depressed. Feeling completely inadequate. In a worship service in a simple Haitian church in the mountains, I realized the depth of the problems. I realized the breadth of the problems. So many hungry people. So many sick people. So many unemployed people. So many hurting people. No infrastructure, no electricity, no running water. Terrible, terrible roads. The hopelessness and the darkness and the almost total lack of opportunities. And I am merely one person. And we are merely one organization.

And I am reminded that it's not just Haiti. Before we turn off our computer, or our smart phone, or our tablet, and before we go to bed in one of our 4 or 5 bedrooms or before we drive off in one of our family's 3 or 4 or 5 vehicles or before we go on vacation, let's think about the rest of the world for a moment:

- 1 billion people are chronically short of food, many slowly starving to death
- 1 out of 4 of the world's 2 billion children are underweight or stunted
- 783 million people have no access to clean water
- One-third of the world's population live on less than $2 a day
- Three-quarters live on less than $10 per day
- 19,000 children under the age of 5 die every day of preventable causes
- And then there are wars and human trafficking and AIDS and cholera and tuberculosis

"There is no way I can solve all these problems," I thought. "I cannot possibly help all these people."

Then it hit me. I don't have to. I am not alone. Our God has His people all over the world. And they are doing great work. They are meeting needs. And helping people and loving people and feeding people. They are providing housing and clean water. They are fixing roads and providing electricity. They are creating jobs. They are operating medical clinics and dental clinics and hospitals. They are caring for children in orphanages. They are sharing the good news of the gospel of Jesus Christ. They are telling about a God of love and care and hope and forgiveness and acceptance and redemption.

And they are doing it with no great fanfare. With no report on the nightly news. You'll never meet them. People like Paul and Kate, a young couple I met last week in Haiti who run an orphanage and a school and a clinic in Port-au-Prince. Or Dianah and Missy who work with a group south of Port-au-Prince that gives dignity and hope to special needs children, a group that has been totally forgotten in all the other challenges of Haitian life.

Or Dwight, who gave the last 30 years of his life starting churches and holding clinics and giving away food and medicine and hope and love and jobs in Honduras. Just because that's what God wanted him to do.

Turns out they're everywhere, these Christians. These Jesus-followers. They're giving and going and sacrificing. They're in South America and Africa and Asia. They've planted themselves in some of the worst places in the world. They're shining a bright light in a dark world and they're making a HUGE difference. A GINORMOUS difference!

And then there are oodles of others, more God-lovers, who go one week at a time. And when they're here in the comfort of the U.S. they are thinking and praying and planning and plotting how to help more, how to go more, how to give more, how to make an even bigger difference. They're using their skills and their education and their experiences and their resources to make a very real and very tangible difference in a hurting world. They're not waiting for someone else to do it. They're figuring it out. They're researching. They're joining with other groups and other Christians and improving their efforts. Because they can. And they're willing to do so. And they're having a blast!

In the end, God was right after all. The Body of Christ has many parts—heads and hands and feet—and when those parts accept their roles and do their jobs and work together, it's amazing what can happen.

So what about you? Are you making a difference in the life of one of God's hurting children? Or are you just living for you and yours, acquiring more stuff, paying more bills, and just going through life as though there really aren't hundreds of millions of people who are hurting and suffering and whose lives could be changed if you got in the ball game?

Come on, Christian! God has blessed you too much, you have too much to offer, and the opportunities are too great for you to sit on the sideline. Get up! Get going! Get involved in the messiness and the trials and the hurts of other people's lives. It will be hard. There will be countless setbacks. But it will be worth it. I can guarantee you. It. Will. Be. Worth it!

It's horrible. It's terrible. It's completely debilitating. And most of us don't get it. Most of us don't understand it. And I suppose that's a good thing. Because if we really understood it, if we really grasped it, that means we would have lived it. And that would be bad.

What is it? It's poverty. Bone-crushing, soul-killing, humanity-denying poverty. Poverty that leaves human beings hungry and homeless and hopeless. Poverty that brings shame and disgrace. Poverty that breeds despair and destruction.

And maybe that's why God has spoken to this issue so much. Maybe that's why King David said, "Defend the weak and the fatherless; uphold the cause of the poor and the oppressed." Maybe that's why James said, "Religion that God our Father accepts as pure and faultless is this: to look after widows and orphans in their distress." Maybe that's why Jesus said, "I was hungry and you gave me something to eat, I was thirsty and you gave me something to drink, I needed clothes and you clothed me, I was sick and you looked after me. Whatever you did for the least of these, you did for me."

Oh, I know. We can't help them all. We can't feed them all. We can't house them all. But we can help some. We can feed some. We can house some. We can encourage and lift up and provide skills and jobs and opportunities. We can do something.

I know we can. I've seen it. I've seen those living in a squalid tent move into a new home. I've seen those starving eat a good meal. I've seen those in desperate need of medical care receive treatment from a doctor. I've seen it over and over again. And it's good. Oh so good.

And there's something else I've seen. Over the last four years, I've had the privilege to speak in many different churches and I've learned that God's people have great hearts. They want to love their neighbors, especially neighbors who are stuck in hopeless poverty. They want to use their blessings to bless others. They want to love the hopelessly poor, not merely in word, but in deed. They do. They really do.

The problem is that often they don't know what to do or whom to trust. But when they know, when they can plug in, when they can give and go and pray and pursue, then watch out! The Bride of Christ is a powerful sort of thing. The Bride is beautiful and good and hopeful. The Bride is a worker and a doer and a prayer. The Bride is a powerful force for good. A powerful force for sharing the love of Christ.

And in a wonderful kind of way, the Bride is very diverse. She consists of plumbers and preachers, doctors and dentists, farmers and pharmacists. The Bride includes coaches and contractors, electricians and engineers. The Bride has young people and retirees. The Bride involves the smart and the talented and the skilled and the gifted. The Bride has financial resources and spiritual resources and people resources. The Bride has much to offer.

And I know this very moment there is a little boy or a little girl who is sitting in a mud hut or huddled in a street alley and thinks he or she doesn't matter. Thinks no one cares. And those little children have no idea where their next meal will come from or whether they'll be able to go to school and learn to read and write and do math and science. They know nothing of a warm bed and a full stomach and a challenged mind. They think a happy home and a healthy home are for others.

And just maybe one day God's going to use you and He's going to use me and that little boy and little girl will experience love and security and all that is needed to grow strong and healthy. And just maybe he'll learn there is a God and she'll learn there is a Savior, and they'll embrace Him and know Him. And their lives will change. Forever. And they will be blessed. And we will be blessed more. And that will be good. Very, very, good.

Right on time. Again. You'd think I would stop being surprised. But I'm not. Thank goodness. We've seen it over and over. Saw it again this week.

We were having trouble with one of our generators. They're made by a great company in Mississippi called Taylor. We tinkered with it and did what we could but weren't exactly sure what to do.

Then the next team from the USA showed up on Saturday. Guess who was on that team? A guy who works for Taylor. And not only does he work for Taylor, he builds generators. It would be absolutely, totally, completely impossible to have a better person to travel to Haiti from America at that specific point in time to help with the generators.

Reminds me of the time we needed cabinets to be built in the first missionary house. We weren't sure what to do. Then God did something that was over the top. We found out that a man on the very next team was President of the National Cabinetry Association. That's right, PRESIDENT OF THE NATIONAL CABINETRY ASSOCIATION! You couldn't make this stuff up. That man came and installed the cabinets that are used every day. And by the way, I talked to him yesterday and he's coming the first week of August to install the new cabinets and countertops in our second missionary house!

Time and time again, we have seen God provide the right person at the right time. Electrical problems? This guy is an electrician. Plumbing issues? This man has been plumbing for years.

Then there was one of my favorites. We were building the church. It's 50' by 30'. That was the largest building we had built. The 30' span was the widest roof we had attempted. We were at that point where it was time to build the roof. Safety is, of course, the number one factor. Who "just happened" to be on a trip with us to Haiti that week? The President and CEO of one of the largest construction companies in the country. Builds skyscrapers and hospitals and megachurches and airports and all sorts of really large buildings. He wasn't overwhelmed by our little 50' by 30' building. He had some great thoughts about our roof construction as well as other aspects of the church. Talked with our builder and we moved forward. You can worship in that building today.

I was reminded this morning of that great hymn we sang so often when I was growing up:

I stand amazed in the presence of Jesus the Nazarene,
and wonder how he could love me,
a sinner, condemned unclean.
How marvelous, How wonderful,
And my song shall ever be.
Oh how marvelous, Oh how wonderful,
Is my Savior's love for me.

Indeed, I stand amazed in the presence of the Living God when I think of all the times He has provided the right person at the right time to enable us to do the work He has called us to do.

My prayer is that as you live your life by faith, you too are experiencing God work in your life in marvelous ways. Remember, if you always have to know every detail of how every situation is going to work out before you take the next step, that's not faith. That's sight. Sight is not all bad, but it's just not faith. And the Scriptures remind us that without faith, it is impossible to please God.

And I would also remind you that without faith, you'll never see God do extraordinary things in your life. So stop limiting God. Trust Him. Exercise faith. Don't forget that God is more interested in your faith in Him than what you might do for Him.

So go ahead. You can trust Him. He'll be right on time.

Been reading a fascinating book entitled *Kisses from Katie* about a girl who graduated from high school and, instead of going immediately to college, sensed a call from God to move to Uganda for a year. A year turned into several years and she is still living in Uganda and is the mother of 14 adopted children. One thing she wrote in her book really grabbed my attention. She stated:

"Matthew 10:28 tells us not to fear things that can destroy the body but things that can destroy the soul. I am surrounded by things that can destroy the body. I interact almost daily with people who have deadly diseases. I live in a country with one of the longest-running wars. Uncertainty is everywhere. But I am also running from things that can destroy my soul: complacency, comfort, and ignorance of those who are suffering. I am much more terrified of living a comfortable life in a self-serving society and failing to follow Jesus than I am of any illness or tragedy."

That last sentence was very powerful to me. How many of us settle for "living a comfortable life in a self-serving society" while "failing to follow Jesus"? My fear is that I would live this one life I have and strive for nothing more than that. Nothing more than being comfortable. Nothing more than the superficial. Nothing more than making sure I was comfortable and happy, all the while missing out on the deeper things of life. Missing out on opportunities to live my life for the glory of God and the benefit of others. Missing out on growing and stretching and reaching and dreaming. Missing out on being a blessing in the lives of hurting people who may not have been fortunate enough to have access to the same education, family, freedoms, resources, and gifts that I have been blessed with.

Katie is a great inspiration. Check out her book. You'll be encouraged, blessed, and challenged to live a life that matters. Before it's too late.

I don't know how your day went yesterday but mine was pretty amazing. It was amazing because of some amazing people. Amazing Christian people.

There are some folks who don't seem to like Christians. They talk about them and say they're mean or angry or rude, and maybe there are a few like that, but I don't know many of them. The Christians I know are good and kind and selfless. They go and do and sacrifice and put others above themselves.

Yesterday, I had lunch with some Christians who told me they wanted their church to take on a big project in Haiti and try to help some of the poorest people in the world. They're not sure about the exact nature of the project, but they know they want to invest much time and much energy and many resources. I heard them talk with both passion and compassion. And they didn't want anything in return. Nothing. They just wanted to use their gifts and their blessings and their resources to share the love of God with others.

Then I talked with another Christian man and he told me that he and his Christian friends want to build a playground and a soccer field for Haitian children. And they don't want anything in return either. They just want to love people in the name of their Jesus. They just want to share their resources with people who have almost nothing. Simply because they care.

And then later last night, I found myself standing in a circle in the home of some other Christian friends. And there were 10 or 12 Christians in this circle, plus my Haitian friends (Pastor Mathurin and his wife, Genese). And these Christians prayed for us. They really, really, prayed for us. And what was so amazing was that one of the people in the circle was recently diagnosed with MS and another person in the circle has a husband who was recently diagnosed with malignant melanoma. And they were praying for us.

And every day, I encounter Christian people just like these. Christians who want to love and share and bless and use their time and resources to love others. They want to make a positive difference in the lives of hurting people. And they want nothing in return. Nothing.

Yes, I like Christians. I like them a lot.

They started walking at noon on Saturday. Just two days ago. They left their crude mountain home because she had been struck in the head by a boulder. She was bleeding profusely. They walked continuously until it became dark and a storm erupted. Some kind people allowed them to stay the night in their mountain home, likely made of mud and sticks.

Yesterday morning, they started walking again. At 9:00 a.m. they finally made it to The Hope Center and our medical clinic there in Haiti. Tony, our full-time American nurse practitioner, tended to her wounds, cleaned off the blood, and stabilized her. He then realized her needs were greater than what we could provide because she had lost a tremendous amount of blood from the blow to her head and from walking for a day. So he drove her to a hospital in Port-au-Prince, paid for her medical care, and headed home.

At 6:00 p.m. yesterday, the husband and wife and four-year-old girl arrived at The Hope Center. They live far in the mountains, a hard drive of 2 ½ hours from The Hope Center. A large tree limb had fallen on the girl, broken her arm, and gashed her head. They had used all their money to go to a trauma center in Port-au-Prince. The good doctors at the trauma center treated her arm but said they do not treat head wounds. Near the trauma center was a man who lives near The Hope Center. He told the little family about our clinic and gave them just enough money to get transportation.

Tony put 20 staples in the little girl's head. Then they told Tony they had no money and nowhere to go for the night. For the first time since April 7, we have no American team staying at The Hope Center. Tony invited them to take a shower, eat dinner, and spend the night in our dorm. They graciously accepted the offer. This morning Tony gave them money to get transportation home.

Between these two medical events, 6 precious children moved into our orphanage. They will not only get a good and safe roof over their heads, but they will receive medical care, dental care, clean water, plenty of food, clothing, a church, a new playground, and scholarships for school. They will learn about a wonderful God who loves them. And they will be loved. Every day.

Stan Buckley

I was thinking this morning that I am so glad our medical clinic is there. I was thinking how glad I am for the new orphanage. And I was wondering. I was wondering if God smiled as Tony cleaned wounds, gave transportation and money for more medical help, and sewed the head of that little girl. I was wondering how pleased God was as that family who had nothing took their showers, ate their meals, and slept on clean sheets.

And there was one other thing I was wondering this morning. As God watched Tony yesterday, did He think about that Samaritan who was so good? I know I did.

He is 88 years old. His name is John. He is sharp and wise and delightful.

I sat next to John last night at dinner . . . in Haiti. At the age of 88 he was on his 4th mission trip to that desperately poor country.

It was John's turn to do the devotion last night. He talked about miracles. He moved from Amarillo, Texas to upstate New York when he was 16. There, he met a girl who would be his wife for 64 years until 2 years ago when God took her home. He thought it was a miracle that he would move across the country as a teenage boy and meet someone with whom he would be so compatible with for a lifetime.

He looked at what But God Ministries is doing in Haiti. He thought it was a miracle how a community in Galette Chambon in the middle of nowhere was birthed from nothing and was giving hope to thousands.

But he said the greatest miracle of all was that his Savior would forgive a sinner like him and give him salvation and make him a child of God.

It was a good devotion. But then it got better. John pulled out a piece of paper and began to sing. He sang every verse of "The Old Rugged Cross". And tears flowed. And it was beautiful.

He is 88 years old. His name is John. And I'm so glad God put me next to him at dinner last night in Haiti.

Don't you hate it when someone challenges that which is near and dear to your heart? I love the church, yet I read the following this morning:

"When historians look back in 100 years, what will they write about our nation of 340,000 churches? Will they look back and see a church too comfortable, insulated from the pain of the rest of the world, empty of compassion, and devoid of deeds? Will they write about a people who stood by and watched while a hundred million died of AIDS and fifty million children were orphaned, of Christians who lived in luxury and self-indulgence while millions died for lack of food and water? Will schoolchildren read in disgust about a church that had the wealth to build great sanctuaries but lacked the will to build schools, hospitals, and clinics? In short, will we be remembered as the church with a gaping hole in its gospel?" - Richard Stearns, *The Hole in Our Gospel*.

I immediately get defensive when I read something like that. Then I have to ask how much of our churches' time and money are spent on us. On those of us who are already saved. Already living in luxury. Already have everything we could ever want. Really, how much? What percentage?

I read this morning in Matthew 11:4-6 that Jesus had been spending time and energy with the blind, the lame, the leprous, the deaf, and the poor. Are those the people, or the types of people, on whom those of us in the church spend our time and energy?

What if we did something really radical and spent far less time and resources on those of us who are already in the Kingdom and who already have everything we need and marshaled our vast resources (both human and financial) to do what Jesus did—preached to the poor, spent time with the outcasts, helped the hurting?

These types of thoughts make me uncomfortable. But perhaps I need to be uncomfortable. For a change.

I hope not. It would be terrible. Really terrible. I would feel bad. Worse than bad. Ashamed. What if I attended classes or services at my church and those classes or services were not pleasing to God? What if they did more harm than good? It can happen, you know.

In fact, there was this church that met all the time. Constantly. But their services were not pleasing to God. They were so bad that a guy named Paul wrote them a letter in which he said, "I have no praise for you, for your meetings do more harm than good."

What were they doing that was so bad? They were fighting and fussing. They were divided. They were selfish. They dishonored God with their attitudes and actions.

So I'm thinking about that church and I'm thinking how horrible those people must have been. I'm thinking they had the opportunity every week to gather with other believers and encourage one another, teach one another, love one another, and work together for the cause of Christ. And they didn't. They just didn't.

And I'm thinking I don't want to be like them and I don't want to be part of a church like their church. Because it would be wrong. And foolish. And dishonoring to God. And I only have a little bit of time on this planet and none of that time should be wasted on things that are wrong and foolish and dishonoring to God.

I hope I never attend classes or services that do more harm than good. Because that would be terrible. Really terrible.

Sitting down this morning. Reading the Bible. Just wondering how much of our time and efforts and resources are spent on those matters that are definitely taught, or even mentioned, in Scripture and how much of our time is spent on issues never mentioned in Scripture. Matthew 15:9 really has me thinking about this. Jesus said, referring to the religious leaders of His day, "They worship Me in vain; their teachings are but rules taught by men."

In other words, they talked about matters that God did not address. Matters in which God was not interested. Matters that they had made up and given a sense of importance even though their directives were not from God. It was just "stuff" they decided was important when, in fact, God didn't care anything about it. And, ultimately, it didn't matter whether anyone adhered to their rules or not. It was pointless. A glorious waste of time.

So, in light of what Jesus said, we have to ask ourselves how much of the conversations in our churches have to do with "rules taught by men" and how much of our conversations are concerned with the actual things of God as related in the Scriptures? In other words, do we talk more about the Bible or more about "church stuff" such as rules and people and gossip and the carpet and the use of the Family Life Center and which songs are sung and who gets to be the third vice-president of the welcoming committee and which programs we are implementing and what color dress she wore and whether he had on a tie? Really, what percentage of our time is spent on these types of matters?

And how much of our conversations are devoted to Scripture and preaching and teaching and missions and sharing the gospel with the lost and encouraging one another and meeting the needs of hurting people and discipling believers and having sweet fellowship with one another? How much of the conversations in our churches are related to things that really matter, that really make a difference in people's lives?

And one more thing. It's a lot more fun and unifying and exciting and rewarding to spend time on the God stuff. So let's choose the God stuff and leave the other to someone else. We'll be a lot happier and God will be pleased. That's a great combination!

I liked it. Wasn't sure I would. But I did. It was church . . . in a bar. Years ago it was a warehouse. Somebody turned it into a bar. Seems like the devil has it Monday through Saturday. But on Sunday, it's holy ground. God's people meet with one another and with Him. Yesterday, several hundred of us met. Mostly young people, twenty-something's. My son, a student there in Nashville at Belmont University, attends every week. He really likes it. That makes me like it too.

We sang some songs. Actually, we sang lots of songs. I didn't know any of them. Not one. But those Jesus-worshipers knew them all. And they sang. Loudly and with passion. You know, hand-raising and that kind of stuff.

The Main Preacher wasn't there yesterday. May have been on Spring Break. So the Associate Guy filled in. They're trying to go through the whole Bible in a year so he picked up where the Main Preacher left off last week. He covered Exodus 19 and 20. Talked about the Ten Commandments. He was good. I was reminded and challenged and encouraged.

We had the Lord's Supper at the end. They didn't do it right. Instead of passing the bread and juice, we had to get up and walk to one of several tables set up around the bar/warehouse/church. Turns out they do this every week.

Oh, they talked about missions, though they didn't call it that. Next Sunday, they have a special offering that will go to 5 projects—water wells and Bibles and churches overseas and inner-city work in Nashville. I really liked that.

Looking back, they didn't do church the way I've always done it. But the songs were biblical and the sermon was biblical, loving others was emphasized, and the people worshiped. Don't know if I would join that church if I moved to Nashville. But I might attend sometime. I liked it. And I'm pretty sure God did too.

I don't want to be like them. They were prideful. They were arrogant. They were angry. They were no fun to be around. They sapped life and energy and hope from everyone they met. Their rules were heavy weights placed on the backs of others. And He didn't like them.

Who were they? Religious people. Very religious people. Went to church every week. Taught Sunday School. Took up the offering. Chairmen of the important committees. You know, personnel and finance. They were very religious. And He wasn't impressed.

I suppose that's one reason they didn't like Him. Because He wasn't impressed. And they wanted Him to be impressed. They really, really, really wanted Him to be impressed.

A doctor named Luke wrote that they "were looking for a reason to accuse Jesus, so they watched him closely." They were religious people looking for a reason to accuse Jesus. Hoping He would do something wrong. Hoping He would mess up. Hoping he would break one of their rules.

It seems that sometimes I fall into that same trap. I'm religious like they were. I go to church a lot. Pray before meals. Teach from the Bible. The same stuff they did. And sometimes I get angry like they did. Angry at all the people breaking the rules. Angry at people who won't conform. Angry at people who don't think like I think. Angry, angry, angry.

And then I find myself looking for a reason to accuse. Looking for a reason to pounce. Looking for a reason to be angry.

Maybe it would be better if I were looking for a reason to bless. Looking for a reason to encourage. Looking for a reason to befriend. Maybe if I were looking for a reason to understand and listen and pray, then maybe I could have a relationship and I could share and tell and inform and let God do the rest. I could let God work on their hearts and their minds and their souls. Because that's what He does.

Should I still have standards? Of course. Should it still disturb me when people flaunt the ways of God? Absolutely. Am I opposed to that which is ungodly and unbiblical and wicked? Very much so.

But in my personal interactions with people, I don't want to be like them. I don't want to be suspicious and angry and paranoid. I don't want to be always attacking and blaming and pointing my finger. I just don't. I don't want to be like them.

No wonder it grew. And grew. And grew and grew and grew. It couldn't help but grow. It was inviting and warm. It was attractive. It was a people and a place where those who came were loved and accepted and blessed. It was full of meaning and purpose and truth. It was a beautiful scene. Not perfect, but wonderfully beautiful.

The early church, the one in Jerusalem, grew at an enormous rate shortly after Jesus went back into heaven. What was it about that church? Why were so many people interested? Maybe the answer is found in Dr. Luke's description of that church. He said they were devoted to sound teaching. They ate together and prayed together and saw God do amazing things. They shared with one another, even sold some of their belongings and gave to those who were in need. Their hearts were glad and sincere. They praised God and enjoyed spending time with one another. Apparently they loved one another. Is it any wonder they grew? How could they not grow?

I don't think that new church would have grown if they had spent most of their time fussing about the color of the carpet or who's on which committee or which song they were going to sing. No one would have been drawn to that. And it's funny, no one is drawn to that today. Turns out people have enough conflict and foolishness in their jobs and their families. They're not interested in going to a church where there is more conflict and more foolishness. And who can blame them?

Perhaps if more of our churches stopped worrying about all those things that don't matter and started focusing on Him and others, then maybe our churches might grow like that church in Jerusalem. In a world filled with hurt and pain and loneliness, people might be interested in a place of love and peace and joy. It worked one other time. Maybe it would work today.

They missed Him. He was right there, but they missed Him. He was in their midst, but they missed Him. He did astounding things, but they missed Him. Given the greatest opportunity in the history of the world, they missed Him.

How strange it seems they would miss Him. After all, He was right there. Literally. They could see Him and hear Him and even touch Him. But they missed Him.

Why did they miss Him? They were blinded. They were blinded by the rules they had invented. They were blinded by the traditions they had embraced. They were blinded by debates in which they engaged.

And they became angry. Instead of being amazed at His power and His love and His wisdom, they became angry. He wouldn't conform to their ways of thinking or doing or being, so they got angry. They really did. I read about them this morning, in Mark 2.

Who were they? They were the church people of their day. They never missed. They were there on Sunday morning and Sunday night. They even went on Wednesday night. They taught the classes and worked on the committees. But in all their busyness, they missed Him. The God they claimed to serve was standing before them and they missed Him.

The hungry and the hurting and the helpless? They didn't miss Him. They saw Him. They embraced Him. They didn't try to make Him conform to their image of who they thought He should be. They didn't try to invent ways and rules and regulations about how to embrace Him or how to see Him. They just embraced Him. Followed Him. Celebrated Him. And He loved them. Boy, did He love them.

I hope I don't do what those church people did in His day. I hope I don't get so caught up in all the rules and all the meetings and all the trappings of modern religion. Because I don't want to miss Him. I just don't.

It wasn't what I thought. I had imagined He would have been hanging out with some really powerful or popular or wealthy people. Most of us would if we could. And He certainly could have done just that. But I discovered in my reading about this Jesus from Nazareth in the first 9 chapters of Matthew that He spent time with those who were ill with diseases, those with severe pain, those with seizures, the demon-possessed, and the paralyzed. And that was just in one paragraph in chapter 4.

In chapters 8 & 9, He spent time with a man with leprosy, a friend's mother-in-law, two more demon-possessed men, a paralyzed man, a bunch of sinners, a dead girl, a sick woman, two blind guys, and a mute. Almost sounds like a bad joke. Where can you find such a pitiful group of people? Turns out, they're everywhere. And they flocked to Him. And He didn't turn His nose up at them. He didn't make them feel worse than they already felt. He didn't shun them or avoid them or run away from them.

Instead, He treated them with love and respect and dignity. He met their needs. He included them. He spent time with them. He valued them. And I must admit that in some ways I'm kind of glad. After all, I am one of those people, or have been, or will be. It's good to know that He will continue to love me even when others don't. Even when I am no longer presentable in proper society. Even when I hurt. Even when I sin. Even when I don't fit in with the rest of the respectable folks.

Well, I'm going to keep reading about this Jesus guy from Nazareth, and if He keeps on hanging out with these same kinds of people, I'm going to have to ask myself if I should do the same. Maybe he will change courses over the next few chapters and then I won't feel compelled to love the unlovely and the riff-raff. I can continue to pretend they don't exist. I won't have to get my hands dirty or get entangled in their complicated, twisted, self-destructive lives. I can live a sanitized kind of life where I block out the unpleasant things of life. And the unpleasant people. It'll be easier that way. Not very fulfilling, of course. But easier.

I'm reading. I'm reading and reading and reading. I'm reading because I want to know. I really want to know. Who is this guy? What's the big deal? Why the big fuss? And there is a big fuss. A huge fuss. The biggest fuss ever. In fact, He has a rather large following. I saw that some singer named Katy Perry has over 60 million followers on Twitter. He has more followers than that. Lots more.

How did He get so many followers? I think I found out when I was reading what His friend Matthew wrote about Him. He did two things. He cared about hurting people and He reached out to bad people to show them a better way. That's what He did. You can read it for yourself. Matthew wrote about some of the times He cared for the hurting—people who were blind, paralyzed, had a fever, had lost loved ones. He helped them and cared about them and took an interest in them.

And then there was that time a bunch of bad people showed up where He was having dinner. And He didn't leave. And He didn't get mad at them. And he didn't throw them out. He just had dinner with them.

So that was His secret. He cared about hurting people and He reached out to bad people to show them a better way. And the hurting people and the bad people loved Him for it. They responded to His care and to His reach.

Maybe He was on to something. Maybe He figured it out. Maybe there's something to this idea of caring about hurting people and reaching out to bad people to show them a better way. Just maybe.

I love that song. At least I used to. Now I'm not so sure. You see, I've always sung it with gusto, singing loudly and really meaning it. Until the other day when I thought about those words.

I'd rather have Jesus than silver or gold.
I'd rather be His than have riches untold;
I'd rather have Jesus than houses or lands;
I'd rather be led by His nail-pierced hand

Than to be the king of a vast domain
And be held in sin's dread sway;
I'd rather have Jesus than anything
This world affords today.

While driving down the road and listening to a really cool version of this song, I realized something. I have just a tiny amount of silver and gold. I certainly don't have riches untold. Houses or land? Just one house and the bank owns part of it. No land. I'll never be the king of a vast domain. Or even a small domain.

The more I sang the song, the more I realized how easy it is to choose Jesus over stuff you're never going to have. There's no sacrifice for me to say that I'd be willing to give up things I don't have or will never have. But could I sing with the same gusto . . .

I'd rather have Jesus than the house I live in.
I'd rather have Jesus than the income I have.
I'd rather have Jesus than the vehicles I drive.
I'd rather have Jesus than the money I possess.
I'd rather have Jesus than the degrees I've earned.
I'd rather have Jesus than the retirement funds I've saved.

Now it gets personal. Now it gets real. No longer is it big and grand and theoretical. If I had to choose, would I rather have Him than those things I have worked very hard to possess? Do I value Him enough to relinquish my iron-fisted grip on the things I do have? Is He more valuable to me than all of that? Is He worth it? All of it?

I'd like to think so. And I'd like to find a song that speaks of sacrificing those things we already possess. And then I'd like to ride down the road singing a really cool version of that song. And I'd like to sing it with gusto.

Don't forget. Whatever you do, don't forget. Don't forget what it was like. Don't forget the pain. And the anguish. And the betrayal. Don't forget.

And the physical pain. It was awful. Just awful. Don't forget the pain. As you go through your day, doing this and doing that, busy as a bee, don't forget.

Tonight I'm going to remember. I'm going to get together with some friends and we're going to remember. We're going to remember what He did, how He suffered, how He bled. And how He died.

We're going to take the bread and we're going to eat it and we're going to remember His body that was broken for us. We're going to take the cup and we're going to drink from it and we're going to remember His blood that was shed for us.

We're going to remember the sins, our sins, that were placed on Him. We're going to remember that He suffered in our place. We're going to remember that He was pierced for our transgressions and crushed for our iniquities. We're going to remember that the punishment which brought us peace was on Him and it was by His wounds we are healed.

We're going to do this so we don't forget. We just can't forget because He suffered so much. He sacrificed so much. And He did it for us. For my friends and me. For your friends and you. We can't forget. We just can't forget.

Have you found it? Is the search going well? Truly, it can be hard to find. We search here and there. We look this way and that way. And just when we think we've got it, it vanishes. Kinda slippery, you know. Many folks search for years and years and never find it. They waste lots of time and effort and energy but still come up empty. So where do you find it, this thing called life? Where do you find real life, meaningful life, forever life?

I have an idea. What if we look where the Giver of this life said to look? It would seem that He would know the place to look since it was all His idea in the first place. But, of course, that's kind of scary. After all, what if He tells us to look in a place and in a way that we don't like? That makes us uncomfortable. But then again, we haven't found it after years of looking on our own, so we should probably try His way.

So, what did He say? Years ago, this Giver of Life, Jesus from Nazareth, said that in order to find life, you must lose it. Weird, I know. How do you find something by losing it? Here's what He said: "Whoever loses his life for me will find it."

Okay, so He said a little more than that. Here's the whole thing: "If anyone would come after me, he must deny himself and take up his cross and follow me. For whoever wants to save his life will lose it, but whoever loses his life for me will find it. What good will it be for a man if he gains the whole world, yet forfeits his soul? Or what can a man give in exchange for his soul?"

What's He saying? He seems to be saying we will never find real, meaningful, purpose-filled life by chasing the things of this world—money, houses, cars, relationships, fame, power, jewelry, success, clothes, accolades.

Instead, we find life by following Him. Seeking Him. Longing after Him. His ways. His teachings. His word. His calling. Him. We die to self, sacrificing what we've always thought was important. In a weird kind of way, by dying we find life. We find life that is filled with meaning and purpose and significance. Life that is rewarding and satisfying. Life that matters. Life that makes a difference. We find what He calls the abundant life.

I know, it sounds odd. Foolish to some. But here's the thing. It's true. It really is. Not always easy, but true. So today, let's start dying . . . so we can really live!

"What's the point? You can't help them all."

"That's just a drop in the bucket."

"There are just too many of them."

We've all heard these lovely words. We've even thought the same things. We try to live out the commands of God in relation to others, but the problems, the obstacles, and the sheer number of people are overwhelming. So what's the answer? If we can't minister to everyone, we should minister to no one?

Then I think about what He did. He helped individuals. Not just nameless, faceless, abstract creatures. No. Real people. With real families and real problems and real hurts. Like the paralyzed guy whose friends lowered him through the roof (that was strange) directly to the feet of Jesus. That guy had a name. He had a mom and a dad. He had friends. Good ones. He had dreams and desires and hopes. And he got healed. Him. Personally. He got up and walked and ran and talked and rejoiced with his family. His life was made infinitely better. His life. And it mattered.

This Jesus seemed to care for the individual. For men and women and boys and girls. For sinners, like that short guy who climbed up a tree (really???) and ended up hosting Jesus for dinner. Jesus went to his house. Sat at his table. Ate his food. And called the religious hypocrites who questioned his actions idiots. OK. So that didn't happen. Just wishful thinking on my part. But the rest is true.

And then there was that time He told those stories about the lost sheep. Just one of 99 was missing. And the lost coin. Just one of 10 was missing. And the people in the stories looked for the one sheep and the one coin. And this Jesus guy said that God feels the same way about lost people. In fact, God is so stoked about lost people being found that Jesus said, "I tell you, there is rejoicing in the presence of the angels of God over one sinner who repents."

So this is really good news. We don't have to help them all. We don't have to minister to every last one of them. Just the ones God puts in front of us. Help one here and help another there. And what's neat is that if I help some and you help some and the other two billion Christians help some, then there would be a lot of people being helped. A lot of love being shared.

And one other thing, if you don't have much influence or much money or much of anything, this helping others deal is just for you. You can take your little influence and your little money and help one little person. In His name. And then, watch how He blesses your efforts in ways you never dreamed possible. Watch how He takes your little and makes much. Watch how He takes your love and your care and your outstretched arms and multiplies it in such a way that you know it was Him and He gets all the glory and you get all the satisfaction.

Happy helping!

It's difficult sometimes. There are trials. And heartaches. There is much I don't understand. Much that doesn't seem to make sense.

Why must the children suffer? Why do bad men seem to prosper? Why is there so much pain and sorrow in this world?

But I hang on. I move forward. I cling tightly to my faith, my Christian faith. My faith in Jesus of Nazareth. After all, where would I go? To whom would I turn?

Would I turn to Hollywood and the shallow, superficial philosophy of hedonism and excess?

Would I turn to politicians and their endless promises and lies and self-promotion?

Would I turn to myself and my own deception and failures and inabilities?

Where would I turn for meaning and purpose and hope? Where would I go for peace and comfort and a future? Who can give me freedom from the overwhelming burden of shame and guilt over the things I have done? To whom would I go?

That's what He asked. Jesus spoke difficult words, challenging words, and the crowd began to thin. So He turned to His close followers and said, "Do you want to leave, too?" And Peter responded with a question, "To whom shall we go?" Then Peter said, "You have the words of eternal life."

We're all following something. We're all following someone. We will live our lives according to some creed or philosophy, whether consciously or not. It may be from our parents or a book or a mentor, but we're all living our lives according to something or someone. We're all looking for meaning and purpose in this life, whether we admit it or not. We just are. And we're all wondering what will happen when we draw our last breath. Is there more? Is there life beyond the grave? We're all wondering and we're all hoping.

And all these years later, Hollywood doesn't have the words of eternal life. Neither do politicians. And neither do I.

That man called Peter was right. Jesus of Nazareth has the words of eternal life. He has the words of hope and peace and joy. He has the words of meaning and purpose and everlasting life. He always has. And He always will.

Just maybe. If they could get close enough. If they could get His attention. If somehow they could break through all the barriers and all the people, and all the rules, then just maybe He could help them.

So they tried. They did all they could do. They shouted and made a scene. It wasn't socially acceptable the way they acted. But what else could they do? They didn't have the inside track. They didn't know anybody who knew anybody. So they yelled out. Really loudly. Just hoping against hope that He might hear them.

Of course, it made everyone else uncomfortable. What were they doing? It wasn't appropriate. There were rules against this sort of thing. Well, not written rules. But there were rules.

And in the confusion He heard them, these two guys. He stopped and He listened. He asked them what they wanted and they told Him. It was pretty big. They weren't merely asking for a handout. They didn't want a temporary fix to a permanent problem. They wanted to see. Literally. They were both blind and they both wanted to see.

You would think that would be a reasonable request. Nothing overly selfish or trivial. But not everyone thought so. Everybody at the scene tried to keep them away from Him. It was so weird. Here was the one guy who could help these men and everyone there tried to keep them away. They told them to be quiet. Just shut up. You're making us uncomfortable.

I am angry at those people. They were mean. And rude. But I'm also kind of sad for them. They didn't get it. They thought He had come for them. And people like them. The decent and the religious and the middle class and certainly the upper class. They thought He was like them. How could He not be?

But they were wrong. He wasn't like them at all. He was royal and divine and the Creator of all things and they weren't any of those things. In a strange kind of way, He was also poor and unemployed and misunderstood and He would be arrested and tortured and killed. They weren't any of those things either. He really wasn't like them.

And there was one other thing about Him. He cared for people like those two guys who were hollering and making that scene. He cared for people they wouldn't have anything to do with. Spent time with them. Went to the houses of the worst among them and sat at their tables and shared a meal. While they were busy erecting barriers for the people who needed Him most, He kept knocking those barriers down and reaching out and loving and caring and giving hope and peace and forgiveness for all their terrible sins. That's what He did.

And what's really sad is that after all these years, we still think He's like us. That He looks like us and thinks like us. He's just one of us. But He's not. He's the Alpha and Omega, the Bright and Morning Star, the Savior of the World, the Holy One of God. And after all these years, He still loves those people. That aren't like us.

Everybody knew it. Everybody. From the little ones to the old ones. They just didn't know when. Or how or where. They knew He was coming but what would He look like? What would He say? What would He do? And how would they know it was Him? There were lots of people walking around. He could be any one of them. Or could He?

He was going to be this great guy. Who did great things. A leader and one to rescue them. They would follow Him. Gladly. But they had to know which one He was. How could they know? Well, as it turns out, years earlier, as in hundreds of year earlier, the ones who had written that He was coming had written what He would be like and what He would do. You know, characteristics. So, if they could just find the guy who matched the characteristics, then maybe that would be Him.

So one day this guy came riding into the capital city on a little donkey. And that was one of those things their writers had predicted. The people went bananas thinking He might be the one. But if that was the only thing He did, He probably wasn't the one. After all, tons of folks rode donkeys. But as it turns out, riding a donkey wasn't the only prediction fulfilled by this guy. There were others. Lots of them. Specific things. Very specific. He did them all.

- Born of a virgin. Check.
- Called Immanuel. Check.
- Great men would adore Him. Check.
- Children of Bethlehem killed. Check.
- Preceded by a prophet. Check.
- Doer of miracles. Check.
- Betrayed by a friend. Check.
- Betrayed for 30 pieces of silver. Check.
- Suffered in silence. Check.
- Nailed to a cross. Check.
- Garments divided. Check.
- Buried with the rich. Check.
- Rose from the dead. BIG check.

So, could He be the one? Could this guy, from that town of Nazareth, given the name Jesus, riding on that little donkey, could He be the one? Could He be the one that was coming to bring hope and peace and joy and life? Could this guy who fulfilled prediction after prediction be the one? Could He?

Well, how could He not be?

They didn't mean it. Well, maybe they did. At the time. They were all excited thinking this was it. Plus, all their friends were excited and it's easier when everybody else has joined in. So they whooped and hollered and got caught up in the moment. Probably got goosebumps, some of them. Everything was going to change for them. He would see to it.

But a few days later, everything had changed. They weren't quite so excited. Actually, some of them were. But excited in a different way. Instead of being for Him, now they were against Him. After all, that's what everybody else was doing. So they got swept up in the emotions and the excitement all over again. It didn't seem to matter the substance. Just went along with the tide. This way one day. That way the next. No anchor to hold when the winds blew.

So they killed Him. Some of them didn't even know why. After all, no real charges had been brought against Him. Certainly nothing worthy of death. Especially that kind of death. But they killed Him anyway. And those who had been in the crowds, the first time and the second time, went home. And I suppose they waited until the next big thing came along. And they got excited all over again.

These people in the crowd live forever. They never seem to die. They're always there. Excited one day, indifferent the next. For Him one day, opposed to Him the next. Certain one day, doubtful the next. Sold out, then burned out. Over and over and over again. Never accomplishing anything. Never going deeper than the moment. Year after year, century after century. The same thing. It must be a horrible roller coaster on which to ride. Of course, I should know. I've bought plenty of tickets for that ride. Maybe I should get off. And decide for myself, without any help from the crowd, who He is. And what He's done. And who I am in light of Him. Maybe that would be better.

What was He doing? What was He thinking? He knew what was going to happen by the end of the week. He knew what would take place.

Me? If I had known? I would have gone someplace else. Any place but that place. Any city but that city. I would have run as far in the opposite direction as my feet would take me.

But not Him. He knew what was coming. The betrayal and the arrest. The ridiculous trials and the hitting and the slapping and the spitting. He knew. The beating and the robe and the thorns. He knew. The nails and the insults. The righteous anger of a holy God. He knew every bit of it. And He rode in on that donkey anyway. And really that's the point, isn't it? He knew and he went anyway. He knew and He faced it. Head on.

I'm really not sure why He went. You know, since He knew. Maybe He went because that was the plan. Maybe because He was supposed to go. Or maybe, because He knew that His death . . . would give us life. He knew.

He was angry. Furious. Not happy at all. He didn't like what He saw. In fact, He hated it. With a passion. A passion that exploded into violence. Well, sort of violence.

Why was He so angry? Because it wasn't supposed to be that way. They had messed it all up. On purpose. It was a special place. Or it was supposed to be.

They didn't care, of course. That special place had become about them rather than about His father and others. Like the poor. And the suffering. And the hopeless. But they didn't care. They were cheating people, robbing them He said. Robbing people who had come for the right reasons. But they didn't care.

So He decided it wasn't OK. It wasn't acceptable. And He did some things and He said some things. He tossed their tables around. Made a mess. Then He told them that special place was supposed to be a place of prayer but there didn't seem to be much praying going on. And He made them leave that special place. Drove them right out.

Oh, and then there's the part we always leave out. After He let his feelings be known, He turned His attention to the blind and the lame. Healed 'em. Loved 'em. Blessed 'em. Sure did. Right there in that special place. The tax collector wrote about it in 21:14. You probably need to read it for yourself since you forgot about it too.

And to top it all off, the little children started shouting His praises. Go read it. They were shouting. Not overly dignified. Probably not following all the rules somebody had made up. But He loved it. LOVED. IT.

But not everybody loved it. You know, all that healing of hurting people and loving on the children. Who didn't like it? The church people. The religious people. The ones who were in charge of that special place, or at least thought they were. The ones who made up all the little church rules but didn't give two mites about hurting people and little children. Well, unless it was their little children and they were dressed up really nice for church. In fact, they hated what He was doing so much that the tax collector said they were indignant. INDIGNANT!

I wonder what He thinks today. You know, when we go to that special place in our community each Sunday and make it about us. When we gossip and act ugly and complain. Usually over nothing. Certainly nothing He cares about.

When we talk about everything—the game, politics—everything but Him. When we get uncomfortable when the guy walks in who's a little dirty. Or the family from the other side of the tracks finally musters the courage to come to the special place and our discomfort is obvious. OUR discomfort. When the whole time we are supposed to be focusing on Him we're focusing on us and our schedule for the next week and all the important things we have to do. When there are 415 million things we could be doing to serve Him and the people He loves but we don't because we're too busy complaining because we didn't like that second song they sang during the service.

I wonder what He thinks. I wonder if He's angry when He looks at what we do at His special place each week. Is He angry? Or maybe just sad.

I can't believe He said it. And neither could they. It was strong, seemingly rude. It was harsh and cutting. But it was true. And they hated it. And they hated Him for saying it.

After all, no one ever spoke to them that way. They were the elite, the educated, the highly religious. Also the pompous. They really believed they were better than everyone else. In a society where religion was everything, they were at the top of the heap. They were the makers of the rules and the keepers of the gate. They were the preachers and the staff members and the deacons and the chairmen of the committees. And not just the flower committee, but the real committees like finance and personnel. They spoke at the meetings and prayed out loud. They preached the sermons and read the reports.

Then He said it. Out loud, in front of others. "The tax collectors and the prostitutes are entering the kingdom of God ahead of you." You could hear the gasp. Tax collectors were traitors to the nation. Cheaters and liars and the worst sort of scum. And prostitutes? They were filthy and worthless and a scourge on society. Was He really saying those people would enter God's Kingdom before the highly religious? Who would think such a thing, let alone say it?

And then He told them why. He told them the tax collectors and prostitutes had repented but they had not. They refused to repent. Their hearts were hard. They simply wouldn't do it.

But really, why should they? Repent of what? They followed all the religious rules. They could quote all the important verses. They had perfect attendance pins from their churches. Plus, they were a whole lot better than tax collectors and prostitutes. I mean, really. Cheaters and harlots. He actually compared them to that riff-raff.

But He was right. He knew their hearts. He knew their lack of justice and mercy and faithfulness. He knew their hypocrisy and their arrogance. He knew they had no love for the hurting and the helpless. It was all one big religious show and He knew it. In fact, a day or two later, He said to them, "You hypocrites! You clean the outside of the cup and dish, but inside they are full of greed and self indulgence. Blind Pharisee! First clean the inside of the cup and dish, and then the outside also will be clean."

But they wouldn't humble themselves and see their own sinfulness, their own hopelessness, their own spiritual poverty. They had forgotten there is no one righteous, not even one. They had forgotten that all their religious deeds were like filthy rags compared to the perfect righteousness of a holy God. They just couldn't understand that all have sinned and come short of the glory of God. All. Every last one of us.

Near the end of that week, He was killed. Sacrificed on a cross for those tax collectors and prostitutes they despised. Yes, they hated the tax collectors and prostitutes, but He loved them and I'm so glad because the truth is I'm like them. After all, I've lied before. I've been less than honest before. Sexual sin? Guilty as charged. You know, that whole lust thing He talked about.

As we draw closer to Good Friday and as we think about His great sacrifice, may God give us hearts that are humble, hearts that are repentant. May He give us eyes to see the truth that we are sinners in desperate need of a Savior. And may we be forever grateful that He was willing to be that Savior for tax collectors and prostitutes and sinners like you and me.

We don't have to wonder. We don't have to guess. It's not a secret. He told us. Not only did He tell us, He showed us.

On that Thursday in that room, He demonstrated once and for all what we are to do, how we are to live. He shared that life would be different in His kingdom. Life with Him would not be about us.

They were a bunch of nobodies. They had neither fame nor fortune. They had no connections, no resources, no power. They had none of the things that make people in our world special or noticeable or important.

And yet the One who had everything, and knew everything, and was everything, took the basin and the towel and washed their feet. Why? Because they were dirty.

And then He told us. He told us how we are to live if we are going to be part of His kingdom. Would it be glamorous? Fancy? Not exactly. He said, "Now that I have washed your feet, you also should wash one another's feet. I have set you an example that you should do as I have done for you."

That's it. Pretty simple. I am to spend my life washing people's dirty feet. And there are dirty feet all around us. There are the dirty feet of failed marriages, poverty-stricken lives, and deadly diseases. There are the dirty feet of unemployment, hopelessness, and mental illness. There are the dirty feet of drug addiction, suicide attempts, and wayward children. Everywhere we look, there are dirty feet that need to be washed clean.

What are we to do? It's no longer a mystery. We are to spend our lives washing dirty feet.

So complicated. So confusing. And so big. Really, who can figure it all out? People, and I mean smart people, spend their entire lives trying to figure it out. They have advanced degrees. Fancy titles. They write books about it. And even they don't understand it all.

But is there any wonder? This thing we call the Bible has 66 different books, written by 40 different authors, over a period of 1,600 years. There's history and law and poetry. And those prophecies. Dragons and beasts and seals and scrolls and bowls and special numbers. Who can figure all that out?

One time I thought I had finally gotten a handle on it, but then I read something that was confusing. Got a commentary and kinda understood. But now I can't recall what I read or what one of those really smart people wrote about it. Back to square one, I suppose.

But then this morning I read what He said. He cut through all the complexities. All the red tape. He went right to the heart of the matter. Reduced it to what matters most. He made it so simple that we can all understand.

A few days before they killed Him, this Jesus—the one who is the center of all the history and all the law and all the poetry and all the prophecies— this Jesus who could have made it even more complicated made it simple for people like you and me. Remember what He said?

When asked which law is the greatest, He said: love God and love others.

OK, so He said it using a few more words. But not many. Here's the quote: "'Love the Lord your God with all your heart and with all your soul and with all your mind.' This is the first and greatest commandment. And the second is like it: 'Love your neighbor as yourself.' All the Law and the Prophets hang on these two commandments."

Really? REALLY? That's it? Seems that way. That's what He said. Boiled it right down to that. Love God and love others. If we would just love God and love others, really and truly and honestly love God and love others, we would be doing all that other stuff the Bible talks about.

Maybe it's not so complicated after all.

Not sure how I feel today. Sad? Angry? Glad? Yes, yes, and yes. They call today Good Friday but was it really? Well, yes, it was for me. And you. And so many others. But not for Him.

It wasn't so good when they slapped Him in the face and hit Him with their fists. It wasn't so good when they lied about Him and mocked Him. It wasn't so good when they beat Him. Almost to death. And it wasn't so good when they drove those nails through His hands and feet. At least not for Him.

That kind of cruelty makes me sad. Who could do such a thing? How could you treat another person that way? Especially One so kind and gentle and wise and pure. It makes me sad to think of how He suffered. For so long. Just hanging there. It makes me sad to think that the wrath of a holy God was poured out on Him for my sins and your sins and the sins of my wife and my sons and my daughter and my parents and the people I go to church with and my neighbors and so many others. That's a lot of sin. That's a lot of darkness. He became all that sin. He embodied it. He took all of it on Himself. And the punishment for all of it was given to Him. Not me. Not us. Him. It makes me so sad.

But it also makes me angry. The cruelty, the lies, the barbaric nature of their actions. It's sickening. And they did it. They gladly did it. I'm angry at all of them. The religious hypocrites. The cowardly Romans. The fickle crowd. The cruel soldiers. All of them! They arrested an innocent man. They beat the One who had done nothing but heal and love and bless. They killed the One who had come to give life. He had done nothing to deserve such treatment. I don't like it and I'm angry about it.

And yet I'm glad. I'm glad it happened. I'm glad He died in my place. I'm glad He paid the price for my sins. Now I don't have to. Now I have forgiveness. Now I have freedom. Now I have hope and a future. Now I have life. Abundant life. Eternal life. I'm glad it happened. Really glad.

It's confusing, these different thoughts and emotions. I want to celebrate what He did that day. I want to rejoice over what He accomplished. And I want to hang my head in shame because my selfish, willful, deliberate, knowing-what-I'm-doing sin helped put Him on that cross.

Maybe I won't try to sort it out all out. Maybe I'll just feel it all. The sadness, the anger, the gladness. Maybe I'll spend part of this day thinking and reflecting and reading and praying. Maybe the worst thing on this day, this Good Friday, would be to feel nothing at all.

I don't know how to do it. I wish I did. But I don't.

He knew how. And He did it. All the time. He loved the outcasts, the poor, and the sinners. Especially the sinners. And not just the misdemeanor type sinners. The really bad sinners. We're talking those with sexual sin. Traitors to their country. Cheaters and liars.

He hung out with them. Even went to their homes. He wasn't uncomfortable around them, He didn't look down on them. He didn't give off a sense of superiority, though He was clearly superior. In every way. Including, and especially, morally superior. After all, He was sinless. So if a guy who was sinless can be comfortable and accepting around a bunch of sinners, why can't a sinner like me do likewise?

Oh, I know. There's that struggle, that never-ending struggle between loving the sinner and hating the sin. But He didn't seem to struggle so much. He just loved people while never compromising.

Maybe He was so comfortable around them because He knew that was His purpose. He knew He had come for them. Specifically. One day all the church people were mad at Him for hanging out with the really bad people and He told them, "It is not the healthy who need a doctor, but the sick. I have not come to call the righteous, but sinners."

Time and again, He could be found hanging out with, spending time with, and caring about people who were living rebellious, sinful lives. And they loved Him. They did. I think it's because they knew He really cared about them. And maybe that's the key. He really did care. He wasn't spending time with them so He could get another notch in His belt, or report it on the church evangelism form, or share a good tear-jerking story during testimony time. He really cared about them. He was interested in them. He wanted better for them. He just loved them.

Maybe we need to get over ourselves. Come down off our high-horse and realize the truth that we are those really bad sinners. Or we were, and we may be again. Maybe we need to start loving people and being comfortable around people and sharing the love He has shared with rotten sinners like us. Just maybe we need to stop worrying what people will say if we're hanging out with sinners and loving them into His presence. And yes, we can do so without compromising and without endorsing and without engaging in the same behavior and all those other excuses we use to not love people who we think are not like us. The people He came for and died for. Those people.

He shouldn't have. The arrest and the slapping and the spitting in His face. He shouldn't have. The merciless beating and the thorns on his head. He shouldn't have. The nails and the bleeding and the suffering and the dying. He shouldn't have.

At least not for me. After all, He knew. Hanging on that cross, He knew all the lies I would tell. All the ungodly thoughts I would think. All the gossip I would repeat. He knew.

He knew all the times I would deny Him. All the days I would ignore Him. All the ways I would disappoint Him. He knew.

He knew about the lust and the jealousy and the anger and the greed and all those things that would one day fill my heart. He knew.

But He bore that cross anyway. He stretched out His arms and He received those nails and He suffered and He bled and He died. For a sinner like me.

This One who was so beautiful and so kind and so caring. This One who loved and healed and forgave. This One who blessed and fed and taught. This One, yes this One, gave His life for me. And for you.

He shouldn't have. He really, really shouldn't have. But I am forever glad He did.

It must have been the sweetest sound she had ever heard. You know, when He called her name. When He said, "Mary."

And it must have been a shock. After all, she had seen Him die. She had seen them place His body in the tomb. And with His death, all hope had been lost. He was gone. This One who had brought such hope and joy and love. This One who had given her meaning and purpose and significance. They had killed Him. For nothing. For no good reason.

And with His death, it was over. Darkness had won. Evil had triumphed. And there was nothing Mary Magdalene could do about it but live in the hurt and the pain and the hopelessness. It was over.

Until that day. Until that first Easter morning when He called her name. And with that, she knew! She knew it wasn't over. She knew there was still hope. There was still joy. There was still meaning to this life and ultimately the life to come.

He was alive! And He would be alive forevermore. No one could hurt Him again. No one could silence Him again. No one could stop Him ever again. And not only that, He was who He said He was. He was the Great I Am, the Son of God. He and the Father were one. He had authority in heaven and on earth. He had authority over death, hell, and the grave. As her friend Peter had said, He was the Christ, the Son of the Living God.

And what He said was true. He would give her His peace. He would give her the abundant life. And He was going to prepare a place for her and all His followers in a magnificent place called heaven. He would come again and take them there. Take them home where there would be no more tears and no more sorrow and no more pain. Where she would see her loved ones and the heroes of her faith. Where she would see the very face of God. He was alive and because He lived, she too would live.

And with His resurrection, hope would prevail. For no matter what happened, it would be okay. When trials came, when finances failed, when enemies struck, when fear attacked, and when death came knocking, in the end it wouldn't matter because evil had done all it could do and it wasn't enough. Death could not contain Him. The grave could not hold Him. He was ALIVE! He was alive, He was alive, He . . . was . . . alive!

And that is why it was the sweetest sound she had ever heard. For you see, my friend, He is risen. He is risen indeed.

He was busy. Very busy. And not with trivial things. He was busy doing important things. Lots of important things. I get tired just reading about His schedule. I'm sure He had a smartphone and two assistants just to keep up with His schedule.

He was here and then there. He was meeting with this group and then that group. He was helping this person and then that person. Always on the go. Always busy. Always the next thing to do.

One day He was speaking in front of a large crowd. Takes lots of energy and concentration to do that. Then He tended to a crazy person. Then He went to the home of a good friend and tended to the friend's loved one who was sick. Then word got out He was there and people from all over brought all their sick and He tended to them. In fact, the whole town came to His friend's house bringing the sick and the hurting and the troubled. He tended to all of them. One person after another after another after another. On and on it went without a break. Loving, sharing, healing, blessing, listening, talking, caring, focusing. Lots of energy expended on that day.

Then suddenly, in the middle of His busyness, He did something unusual. Well, I thought it was unusual. He stopped. He just stopped. Before going to the next appointment, the next meeting, the next whatever, He stopped. And He did two things: He went off to a solitary place and He prayed.

Oh, they didn't like it. The people who demanded His attention didn't like it one bit. In fact, they went looking for Him. But He knew something they didn't know. If He was going to be effective, if He was going to be helpful, if He was going to keep His sanity, then He had to do those two things: go off to a solitary place and pray.

I was thinking that since you are worn out, exhausted, and cranky, and since there's no end in sight to what you've got to do, maybe you should do what He did. After all, if Jesus Christ the Son of God the Doer of Miracles the Creator of all things the Alpha and Omega the Prince of Peace the Holy One of God the Great High Priest the Lion of Judah . . . if the King of kings and Lord of lords needed to go to a solitary place and pray, you probably do too.

Why would they do something so outlandish? What would everyone think? Could be embarrassing. They might even get in trouble.

But they did it anyway. They started digging. That's what it says. They started digging. Not in the ground, mind you. In the roof!

They knew it was his only hope. They knew that no matter what, they had to get their friend to Jesus. They knew that Jesus could give their friend hope and healing and a future.

So they dug through that roof and lowered their paralyzed friend to the feet of Jesus. Of course, He did what He always did. He stopped what He was doing. Turned His attention to the one in need and healed him. Right there on the spot, healed him. The guy got up, took his mat, and walked out in full view of everyone there.

We don't know much about these guys, these friends who dug through the roof. We only know they loved their friend enough to carry him to Jesus.

I wonder who it is that I need to carry to Jesus. Who is that person that has tried everything but can't seem to walk upright in this life? He's tried religion and self-help books and treatments and seminars. But what he really needs, what she really needs, is Jesus. His power, His love, His forgiveness. That friend needs His joy, His peace, His wisdom.

Maybe today I could just tell my struggling friend about Jesus. You know, the Jesus who has touched my life. Who has given me such joy and hope and peace. The Jesus who has given my life meaning and purpose and provisions. The Jesus I have worshiped and loved and walked with and talked with and who has been so real so many times.

I could continue to dispense my advice and my logic and my analysis of my friend's situation. Or, I could just carry him to Jesus.

They were wrong. Dead wrong. They didn't understand, they didn't get it, so they jumped to ridiculous conclusions.

Some thought they were doing the right thing. His family members showed up to take charge of Him. "Out of his mind," they said.

Others never liked Him from the start. They were jealous and defensive and arrogant. They said He was possessed by a demon.

Truth is He wasn't crazy or demon-possessed. But they didn't understand. They didn't get it. So what did He do? Did He cave in, give up, or go home? Hardly. This Jesus guy who was causing such a stir kept doing what His Father had told Him to do. He stayed true to His mission. He continued to hang out with the poor and the desperate and the hopeless. He continued to speak the truth even when those in power didn't like it. He stayed the course even when many didn't understand.

Turns out His plumb line, His measuring stick, His guide-for-life wasn't the opinion of others. It wasn't the mood of the crowd or the currents of culture. It was the will of His Father.

Sometimes it's hard to do the right thing. Or the thing that nobody understands. Or that which runs counter to modern wisdom. Our enemies may talk about us. Our friends may think we're crazy. But sometimes, when our lives line up with the will of the Father, when our lives are consistent with the Word, when our plan is His plan, we do it anyway. Because sometimes they're wrong. Dead wrong.

He was there. Right in the middle of it. In all the pain and all the heartache and all the hurt. In the disappointments and the challenges and the unfairness of it all, He was there. Countless times.

The blind, the deaf, the bleeding, the paralyzed—He was there. The demon-possessed, the guilty, the lonely—He was there. Those with pain and seizures and various diseases—He was there.

Time and time again, He reached out and He helped up those who were struggling through the challenges of life. That's who He was. That's what He did. That Jesus. That beautiful, kind, strong, good, truth-telling Jesus. He was there.

And He's still there. Today. In the midst of pain and suffering and heartache, He's there. He's there in our thoughts. He's there in our hearts. He's there in His word. He's there in you, and me, as we reach out and we help up those who, today, are blind and deaf and bleeding and guilty and lonely.

Oh, I know. He left. In a cloud, no less. But He's coming back. Until that time we have our marching orders. We carry on. The loving, the caring, the reaching out and helping up. We carry on. All for His glory and for the benefit of others. In His name, we carry on.

Who is this? Who. Is. This? We've heard Him, we've watched Him, and now this. The other things He did were pretty good, but this one is over the top. Really, who does this sort of thing?

That day when He told the wind and the waves to be quiet—and they did— that was too much. Until that moment, they knew He was special. They knew He was different. But they had never seen such a display of power. Who was this guy? Who is this?

Turns outs, that's the ultimate question. And it's not enough to say He was a great guy who did some neat things. That's a cop-out. An avoidance. A refusal to man-up and make a choice.

We have to decide. For ourselves. And we all do. After all, He's impossible to ignore, at least forever. He's everywhere. People talk about Him and write books about Him. They have classes about Him. Hundreds of millions even worship Him. At some point we all must decide. Either He's no big deal, an overblown figment of the religious world's imagination, or He's the One. The One to follow. And trust. And believe in.

At some point we make a decision, OUR decision. Not our mom's or our dad's, our pastor's or our grandparent's. WE decide. On our own. So go ahead. Stop and think. Consider. Reflect. Read and study and discuss. It's worth your time. It's more important than your endless, frantic, nonstop busyness that allows you to avoid the deeper things of life.

And one more thing. Be careful. There's a lot riding on how you answer that question they asked so long ago. Who is this?

I like a lot of things Jesus said. I like it when He said that He came to give us the abundant life, that He came to give us His peace, and that He came to seek and save the lost. I like it when He said that God so loved the world that He gave His one and only Son. I like it when Jesus said that if anyone is thirsty, let him come to Jesus and drink.

But there are some things Jesus said that I don't like. I don't like it when He told the guy who wanted to bury his father before following Jesus that the guy should let the dead bury their own dead (seems rude). I don't like it when Jesus said that anyone who looks at a woman lustfully has already committed adultery with her in his heart (I've done that countless times). I don't like it when Jesus said that anyone who divorces his wife and marries another woman commits adultery, and the man who marries a divorced woman commits adultery (seems harsh and a lack of understanding of truly difficult marriages).

I don't like it when Jesus said that anyone who does not hate his father and mother, his wife and children, his brothers and sisters – yes, even his own life, cannot be My disciple (doesn't make sense to me). I don't like it when Jesus said to love your enemies and pray for those who persecute you (some people are rude and mean and I just don't like them). I don't like it when Jesus talked about fasting (I rarely, if ever, do). I don't like it when Jesus said not to judge or we too will be judged (I enjoy judging others and do it often).

I don't like it when Jesus said that it's easier for a camel to go through the eye of a needle than for a rich man to enter heaven (compared to most of the world, I am very wealthy). I don't like it when Jesus said that many who are first will be last, and many who are last will be first (I enjoy being first).

I don't like it when Jesus said that He did not come to bring peace to the earth but that He had come to turn a man against his father, a daughter against her mother, a daughter-in-law against her mother-in-law and that a man's enemies will be the members of his own household (doesn't seem very family-oriented). I really don't like it when Jesus said that I should take up my cross and follow Him (the cross was an instrument of torture and death).

Jesus said some tough things. Some really hard things. It's easier to pretend Jesus didn't say such things. That way I don't have to be challenged in my thinking and my living. That way I don't have to wrestle with difficult spiritual concepts. That way I can sanitize Jesus and make Him in my own image. I can turn Him into this sweet little character that is loved by everyone and would never challenge anyone and never hurt anyone's feelings and who would be okay with everything people say and do. I think I'll just focus on the things Jesus said that I like and ignore the things Jesus said that I don't like. It's easier that way.

He is.

He is Immanuel, God with us.

He is the Wonderful Counselor, Mighty God, Everlasting Father.

He is the Prince of Peace.

He is the Living Water and the Bread of Life.

He is the Lamb of God who takes away the sin of the world.

He is the Lion of Judah.

He is the Word who was with God and who is God.

He is the First and the Last.

He is the Living One who was dead and is now alive.

He is the Rider called Faithful and True.

He is the One with whom the blind receive sight, the lame walk, those who have leprosy are cured, the deaf hear, and the dead are raised.

He is the One who preaches the good news to the poor.

He is the One who took up our infirmities and carried our sorrows.

He is the One who was pierced for our transgressions and crushed for our iniquities.

He is the Christ, the Son of the Living God.

He is Jesus.

That's who He is. And that is enough.

I want to see. That's what he said. More than anything in the world he wanted to see. He didn't ask for a new car or a new house or a fancy vacation. He had one chance to make one request and that's what he said. I want to see.

His name was Bart, or something like that. He was blind. Couldn't see a thing. But he wanted to. He really, really wanted to. And then he got his chance. This Amazing One he had heard about was passing through his town so he took a chance. He cried out to the only One who could help him, the only One who could give him sight.

And that's when it happened. The Amazing One stopped. He called for Bart to come to Him. And Bart did. In fact, Bart threw aside his coat, jumped to his feet, and quickly made his way to the Amazing One.

Sometimes I feel like Bart. Sometimes I just want to see. I've gotten a glimpse before. I know how beautiful it can be. But I want to see clearly. I want to see better and further. I want to see and know and understand. I want to see Him. I want to know Him. I want to experience Him. I want to see truth and honesty and grace and love. I want to see His heart and His mind and His ways. I want to see a life of meaning and purpose and significance. I want to see Him work in me and through me in ways I've never even imagined. I want to see lives changed for His glory and their benefit. I want to see.

Maybe I need to be like Bart. Maybe I need to throw my coat aside and make my way quickly to this Amazing One they called Jesus. Maybe I need to throw aside my pride, my fears, my sin. Maybe I need to get rid of doubt and everything else that is holding me back from quickly and continually going to Him. Maybe, just maybe, I need to exercise faith and courage.

That's what Bart did. He tossed aside his coat and everything else that hindered him from going to the Amazing One. And on that magnificent day, the Amazing One gave him the one thing he desired more than anything else—his sight.

Yes, I think I'm like Bart. On this day, at this time, more than anything else, I want to see.

He told them. He just flat-out told them. Why would he tell them? Because they didn't know. And they needed to know. They really, really, really needed to know. So he told them.

It says he (1) stood up, (2) raised his voice, and (3) addressed the crowd. Not a bad formula.

And what he told them was pretty important. It wasn't the score of the game or the latest celebrity gossip. It was a matter of life and death. Or life and death . . . and then more life.

He told them there was this guy named Jesus who did a bunch of miracles. Then they killed Him. But God raised Him from the dead. This Jesus was both Lord and Savior. That's what he told them.

A lot of them were stunned. They had heard about this Jesus guy but didn't know the whole story. They weren't sure what to do, so they asked. And he told them. Said to turn from their sinful and selfish ways and turn to God. And be baptized. That's what he said. Told them to do it in the name of this Jesus so their sins could be forgiven.

You'll never believe what happened. They did it. Lots of them. Three thousand of them. And so it all began. Two thousand years ago. All because he told them.

I wonder if there are others who need to know. I wonder if I should tell them.

Stan Buckley

They asked Him to leave. Go away. They didn't want to see Him anymore. They didn't want to be in His presence. They just wanted Him to go.

And it seems rather strange. After all, He had done something amazing. They had seen it. There was this man they had known for years who had something wrong with him, something terribly wrong. He wasn't normal. He was crazy. Really crazy. Didn't wear clothes. Lived outside and alone. They didn't know what to do with him so they ignored him, felt sorry for him, and stayed away from him.

Then one day this guy they had heard about came along and encountered the crazy man. He spoke to the crazy man and healed him. Drove the craziness right out of him. Then the crazy man put on clothes, sat down, and acted like a normal person. Like nothing was wrong. He was healed.

When the people saw what had happened to the crazy man, they didn't celebrate. They weren't happy for the man. Instead, they were afraid. They were afraid of the Man who had healed him. So they asked Him to leave. To go away from their town. To move somewhere else. That's what they did. They asked Jesus to leave. And He did.

I've often wondered why they did that. Instead of asking Him to leave, why didn't they ask Him to stay? This doctor named Luke who reported on the story said they were afraid. He said they were overcome with fear.

After thinking about it a while, I think I may understand. Sometimes I do the same thing. Sometimes I ask Him to go away. Because I'm afraid. I'm afraid if I ask Him to stay, He will draw me closer to Himself and reveal things about me that aren't good. Things I don't want to face.

And He might ask me to trust Him. And get out of my comfort zone. And believe more in Him than in me. Along the way, He might ask me to sacrifice and give and go. He might ask me to change my plans and maybe even change my life. And that scares me.

It's easier just to ask Him to leave.

He couldn't explain it. At least not completely. He knew what had happened, just wasn't sure of all the details.

Of course, everyone knew something had happened. It was obvious. And they wanted to know all about it. But he was no wordsmith. No giver of speeches.

But there was one thing he did know. He was blind, but now he could see. That's what he said. Repeatedly. He was blind. Then this guy came along and now he could see.

Oh, they were mad about it. All the scholars and the leaders and the smart people. They wanted a full explanation. They wanted details and a thorough analysis. They were sure something sinister had happened. They weren't in charge of what had taken place so it must have been bad. So they kept asking. Over and over. One question after another.

He finally told them he couldn't answer all their questions. But there was one thing of which he was certain. He was blind, but now he could see.

Turns out this blind guy was not the only one. There have been millions and millions of blind people who have received sight after an encounter with Him. They were blind to truth and hope and goodness. They couldn't see a future or a way out. And then they met Him, Jesus of Nazareth. Their eyes were opened. After years of stumbling in the darkness, they could finally see.

They could see meaning and purpose in life. They could see forgiveness and healing. For the first time they could see love. Real love. Not that counterfeit love that abuses and hurts. But real, no conditions added, love. And like that first guy, they might not be great orators. But there was one thing neither they nor anyone else could deny. They were blind, but now they see.

Seems like sometimes we can't explain everything. Sometimes we can't give the answer everyone wants. And sometimes we don't need to. Sometimes all we can say is exactly what happened. I was blind, but now I see.

Stan Buckley

I like helping people who are nice. And good and kind. Those who are pleasant and grateful. I don't like helping people who are mean or rude. Or lazy or trouble-makers.

I'm glad He's not like me or I would be in big trouble. Eternal trouble. You see, He loved me even when I wasn't good and kind. Or pleasant and grateful. Even when I was mean and rude. And lazy and a trouble-maker. It says in the book called Romans that "while we were still sinners, Christ died for us."

I suppose that means He died for me even though I had a lot of sin in my life. A lot. Sins of the flesh, sins of the spirit. Sexual sin. Pride. Meanness. Theft. Arrogance. Rudeness. Envy. Selfishness. It's all there. Every bit of it.

I wouldn't have died for someone like me. I would've said someone like me doesn't deserve it. Or hasn't earned it. Or should be punished. That's what I would have said.

But not Him. He said He loved people like me anyway. And that people like me, big sinners, need grace and love and forgiveness more than anyone.

So He carried that cross and He paid that price. That awful, terrible price. And it has made all the difference for a sinner like me.

Acknowledgements

I want to thank the Board and team members of But God Ministries. Their amazing work in Haiti and the Mississippi Delta inspires me every day to think, write, lead, and love.

I am forever indebted to my parents, Gerald and Billie Buckley, for their undying love and support during my years of growing up in Natchez, Mississippi. They encouraged me, believed in me, and always told me I could do it.

I must thank Olivia Dear for editing the manuscript. She spent countless hours making this book better than it otherwise would be. I also want to thank Anna Hays with The Omega Group for her patience and her incredible work designing the cover for this book.

I would like to thank my family for their constant love and support. My son, Adam, and my daughter, Anna, have brought me great joy throughout their lives. My son, Neal, has also brought great joy into my life and I want to thank him for helping to edit and categorize hundreds of devotions that make up this book.

Finally, none of this would be possible without the love and support of my wife, Jewell. She has stood firmly by my side through major transitions as I've gone from practicing law to serving as a pastor and then leading a non-profit organization. She has always supported, always believed, always loved.

Printed in the United States
By Bookmasters